THE DRY FLY
AND FAST WATER

HERITAGE SERIES
VOLUME 1

THE DRY FLY AND FAST WATER

Fishing with the Floating Fly on
American Trout Streams, Together with Some
Observations on Fly Fishing in General

by George M. L. La Branche

With an introduction by Paul Schullery
and illustrations by Ernest Lussier

Greycliff Publishing Company
Helena, Montana

10 09 08 07 06 05 04 03 02 01 00 99   10 9 8 7 6 5 4 3 2 1

Cover photograph: ©Richard Franklin
LaBranche fly patterns tied by David B. Ledlie
Fly photographs by Doug O'looney
Designed and typeset in Garamond and Benguiat Gothic by Geoffrey Wyatt, Helena, Montana
Cover design by Geoffrey Wyatt
Printed by BookCrafters, Chelsea, Michigan

Library of Congress Cataloging-in-Publication Data

La Branche, George M. L. (George Michel Lucien), 1875–1961.
    The dry fly and fast water : fishing with the floating fly on American trout streams, together with some observations on fly fishing in general / by George M.L. La Branche ; with an introduction by Paul Schullery ; illustrations by Ernest Lussier.
        p.   cm.
    Originally published : New York : C. Scribner's sons, 1914. With new introd.
    Includes index.
    ISBN 0-9626663-6-X (alk. paper)
    1. Trout fishing—United States. 2. Fly casting—United States. 3. Fly fishing—United States. I. Title.
OSH688.U6L3   1998
799.1'757—dc21   98-16080
                                                                        CIP

CONTENTS

ILLUSTRATIONS

ILLUSTRATIONS CONTINUED

PREFACE

To expound a theory into willing ears upon a trout stream is one thing; to put those same ideas into writing so that they may be intelligently conveyed to one who reads them is quite a different thing. Of this I am convinced. However this may be, my readiness to do the one induced in some of my angling friends the belief that I could do the other. They insisted that I try—and this book is the result. My experience in preparing these pages has filled me with the profoundest respect for those persons who may be truthfully characterised as authors. I began the work with a good deal of timidity, and, as it now appears to me, considerable temerity. After completing the task to the best of my ability I submitted the manuscript to some of my credulous friends. Strange to say, after reading it, even then they insisted that I publish it. By this decision it seems to me they proved two things—their friendship for me and their absolute unfitness to be literary critics. Even so, under their instruction and guidance, the book is presented to the angling public with the hope that it may find some small favour among them.

G. M. L. L.
May, 1914

INTRODUCTION
BY PAUL SCHULLERY

For me, George La Branche's book, *The Dry Fly and Fast Water,* stands for the best and the worst when reading one of fly fishing's authentic classics. When I first began reading fly-fishing books, it was one of the books I was told I must read right away, a real masterpiece, a milestone, a genuine contribution, and so on. So I dutifully read it, tripping over various archaic terminology and outdated tackle discussions, and feeling like I was somehow missing something, which I was.

Reading it now, a couple decades later, I am repeatedly surprised by its authority; it is indeed all of those good things it was claimed to be. But when I first read it, I had so little frame of reference, and so little understanding of La Branche's subjects, that I got little more from it than what I already knew from having read *about* it.

There is in fact much more of value in it than the one- or two-paragraph summaries it receives in popular fishing histories, but twenty years ago when I read it, I was a little like the college freshman who complained that reading Shakespeare was tedious because the old guy used so many clichés. I just had no idea what I was reading. Let us hope that even if you have never read a fly-fishing book before, this introduction will give you some idea of what La Branche was up to, and what he achieved.

Let me begin by establishing, initially, that here is one

of the genuine experts. We've heard enough stories of famous experts who turned out to be all too mortal when actually asked to demonstrate their skills publicly, but it appears that La Branche had no trouble in that regard. First consider the opinions of a couple of his American contemporaries. Here's Sparse Grey Hackle, in *Fishless Days, Angling Nights* (1971):

> George La Branche had the most delicate presentation of any angler whom I have ever observed. In his books, George speaks repeatedly of checking the fly in the air to get a delicate delivery, but what he did was really more than that. He made each cast, short or long, with a deliberate powerful stroke; checked the line hard so that the fly whipped down until it was only an inch above the water, with its headway killed; and then seemed to lower it gently, through that remaining inch, onto the water.

And here is Carl Otto von Kienbusch, creator of the fabulous angling library now residing at Princeton, quoted from an interview in 1974 that was published in *The American Fly Fisher* in 1980:

> George La Branche was always my model as a fly fisherman. He was the finest technician with a fly rod I ever came in contact with. He never cast a long line—only 25 or 30 feet—but he could put the fly in a curve on a penny, and he could catch fish when no one else could.

The problem with these testimonials, you might notice, is that their significance depends in part upon the authority of their sources. Sparse and Kienbusch were admired in their small elite circle of well-heeled anglers, but how does the average reader know if they were any good at catching fish, much less at judging the skills of another fisherman? Luckily, they didn't just praise La Branche as a great fisherman, they described the extent of his skills pretty specifically—casts he could make, that sort of thing.

A potentially more neutral observer, writing in the British *Fishing Gazette*, described La Branche's casting during a visit there:

> This remarkable caster cast the dry fly in places in which it would be extremely difficult to drop a worm, under overhanging alders and blackberry bushes, around trunks of trees, casting at will on particular leaves that the fly might drop thence like a caterpillar from an oak leaf. His fishing is smooth and entirely effortless . . . . Briefly, Mr. La Branche is a very beautiful fisherman.

And then, a brief note from one of the twentieth century's foremost fly-fishing authorities, the great British writer G. E. M. Skues. In a letter written in 1933, describing an outing on the Itchen, Skues gave La Branche this praise:

> Colonel Harding was to have been my guest for my last week-end, but he was laid up with lumba-

British writer G. E. M. Skues (left) corresponded with George La Branche and fished with him when La Branche visited England.
COURTESY OF THE ANGLERS CLUB OF NEW YORK

go and lumbar rheumatism, and at the moment that I heard of this from him I had a call from G. M. L. La Branche, so I got him down instead. It was quite a nice week-end for weather, but I only got one trout and one grayling, and La Branche got one grayling, though he rose and held for a moment a trout of about 1 1/2 lb. on a huge variant with a greenish olive hackle. I could not imagine how he got such a fly to the trout as delicately and accurately as he did.

All the sources, including those who may not have agreed with his theories, give us pretty much the same story. La Branche seems to deserve his legendary reputation as a great fisherman. It will be up the each reader to decide if he was also a great teacher. I think he was.

Who Was George La Branche?

It seems odd that one of American fly fishing's most polished, dapper, and articulate writers, who was described as "the nattiest dresser you ever saw out fishing in your life," and who, when asked if at any time during the Great Depression he was down to his "last million," responded, "Good God, no," started out as a high school dropout.

According to the *National Cyclopedia of American Biography,* George Michel Lucien La Branche was born in New York City on May 25, 1875. The *Cyclopedia* is concise on his rise in business:

His father was an accountant. After attending public schools of his native city, George M. L. La Branche went to work in 1897 for James R. Keene, a stockbroker. Later he became Keene's personal secretary, continuing in that capacity until 1912. Having learned the operations of the

George M. L. La Branche
FOREST AND STREAM, OCT. 20, 1906, COURTESY ED VAN PUT

purchase and sale of securities, La Branche established himself as a member of the New York Club
Market in 1912. Five years later he purchased a
seat on the New York Stock Exchange, and in
1924 he organized La Branche & Co., New York
City, with which he was associated until his
retirement in 1946.

Most of what you might want to know of his early
fishing life and the development of his theories is in the
book you are about to read. He first cast a dry fly, by all
accounts, in 1899, on, according to his book, the pool at
the junction of the Willowemoc and the Mongaup in the
Catskills.

He was not only a superb caster when fishing, but
also competed successfully in casting competitions. His
name shows up in various casting competition records in
the early 1900s. At the 1909 annual meeting of the New
York Angler's Club, he was awarded the "record medal"
for his score of "98 and ⅜ per cent" in the dry-fly accuracy
event. And, though he was not thought of by his fishing

La Branche first cast a dry fly at the junction of the Willowemoc (above) and the Mongaup in the Catskill Mountains of New York.

RECREATION, JULY 1909, COURTESY ED VAN PUT

companions as needing to make even medium-length casts to catch fish, he won the trout-fly distance prize in the 1911 Angler's Club of New York Tournament with a cast of ninety-four feet. Imagine doing that, as he did, in a good suit, with a four-ounce bamboo fly rod, silk line, and gut leader.

It is probably also a testament to his skills that it only took him a few years from the time he first cast a dry fly to become recognized as one of the dry fly's leading practitioners and foremost promoters in America.

THE AMERICAN DRY FLY

Anglers have floated their flies over trout for centuries. In the past twenty years, Jack Heddon and Conrad Voss Bark in England, and Ken Cameron, David Ledlie, I, and a few others in the United States, have taken a hard look at the evidence and decided that the dry fly didn't spring full-formed from the mind of a few Victorian gentlemen; it evolved out of a variety of older practices, in a variety of settings on many waters. By the late 1800s, when Frederic Halford began publishing his landmark series of books on dry flies in England (starting with *Floating Flies and How to Dress Them,* 1886), the sporting press on both sides of the Atlantic contained occasional enthusiastic articles about flies fished on the surface.

At the same time, a growing leisure press and a rapidly changing sporting society combined to accelerate all dialogues relating to the blood sports. Fly fishermen, in particular, were talking to each other more than ever, in person and through their publications, and they seemed to find no end of things to talk about. Dry flies were only a small part of it. Angling entomology, a revolution in rod-building and reel-making, sporting ethics, conservation of natural resources, and many other subjects were debated weekly in the great old periodicals such as *Forest and Stream, American Field,* and *American Angler.*

All of this dialogue accelerated the growth and change of fly fishing, and certainly heightened awareness of the worth of floating flies of one type or another. The quarterly publication of the American Museum of Fly Fishing, *The American Fly Fisher,* has reproduced many of these early floating-fly essays over the years, along with extensive evaluation of them. I've summarized much of this material in my book, *American Fly Fishing: A History* (1987). There is no need to repeat all that here, but you will need some background in how the dry fly got where it is today.

It was not a united movement. As the twentieth century opened, there were already several rather loosely identified schools of thought competing for the approval of potential dry-fly fishermen, especially in America.

One was the British approach, an attempt at a nearly scientific systemization of the needs of anglers. Through familiarity with a growing entomological science, and through employment of new materials, fly rod designs, and fishing codes, followers of Frederic Halford formalized an approach to dry-fly fishing based partly on knowing the insect life and partly on responding to the fishery within a fairly rigid set of manners. One fished a fly designed to imitate a specific insect, one cast upstream, one cast only to rising fish, one fished only on the surface, one imparted no action or motion to the fly.

If you want to take the time, you can discover that not all of Halford's British contemporaries bought everything he said, either about fly patterns or about fishing ethics. Don't let me appear to fall into some new version of the oversimplification trap that has made this story so flat and unstimulating in the past.

Halford and his colleagues were in fact published now and then, sometimes at length, in American sporting periodicals in the 1880s and 1890s. Americans had ample opportunity to know about this new British dry-fly movement.

One of the strangest little quirks of the old view of American fishing history was that it portrayed one man, Theodore Gordon, as single-handedly starting the American dry-fly movement by writing to Halford about dry flies in 1890. I've troubled some Catskill regionalists by demonstrating that it wasn't that simple, and this isn't the place for an extended revival of that debate, but you

Theodore Gordon
NEW YORK HERALD, APRIL 1, 1904, COURTESY ED VAN PUT

need to know a little of it to understand how La Branche fits in this story.

It is true that Gordon wrote the letter, and that Halford obligingly sent him a set of his flies. It is also true that Gordon was enormously important in the development of American dry flies. But the long-popular story then goes on that in this way, because of this correspondence between Halford and Gordon, the dry fly abruptly arrived in America. As John McDonald wrote in his introduction to *The Complete Fly Fisherman* (1947), Gordon's collected notes and letters, "Halford replied . . . enclosing a paper into which he clipped a full set of his dry flies, each carefully identified in pen and ink, and the dry fly winged its way to the New World." This view of American dry-fly history has been parroted countless times since McDonald wrote it.

The story has a nice clarity, but it doesn't make a great deal of historical sense. Gordon, for one thing, wouldn't have known to write to Halford about dry flies had he not heard about them somewhere. We can assume that he read about them in the American or British sporting press, both of which were regularly publishing articles about dry flies, advertisements selling dry flies, and reviews of books that explained how to make and fish dry flies. Dry flies had been winging their way across the Atlantic for years prior to Gordon's letter. American dry flies, which have grown into a far more diverse lot than their British ancestors, do not spring from any one event (and to his credit, Mr. McDonald does acknowledge at least some of the growth of interest in dry flies prior to 1890 in the new introductory material in the 1989 edition of *The Complete Fly Fisherman;* oddly, though, he also lets the earlier statement stand).

Perhaps the foremost proponent of the Halfordian approach in America before 1890 was brought back into the light recently by angling historian David Ledlie. The man was a transplanted Englishman, John Harrington Keene, who came to the United States in the early 1880s. In his books, especially *Fishing Tackle, Its Materials and Manufacture* (1886), *Fly-Fishing and Fly-Making* (1887), and in dozens of articles, he showed how to tie dry flies, and he preached the need for more attention to angling entomology and accurate imitation of American trout stream insects. (And let me beat this particular dead horse a little more here; notice that Keene's books, and many of his articles, were published in America prior to Gordon's famous letter to Halford.)

An innovative creator of remarkably modern flies, and a commercial fly tier who seems to have influenced at least a few commercial fly dealers (including Orvis) in the 1880s and later, Keene ended up feeling mostly ignored by Americans who, raised on brook trout fishing, were reluctant to embrace wholeheartedly the formal, even rigid, approach of Halford. But in the meantime, Keene was widely published, and we can assume he was widely read. So, I assume were the writings of the British dry-fly specialists, whose books were advertised and excerpted in the sporting periodicals.

Numerous Americans in the 1880s and 1890s wrote about dry flies; as I mentioned earlier, several companies offered them for sale, either marketing Halford flies or creating their own patterns. But, as I also mentioned, of all these promoters of the dry fly, only one name made it into prominence in the minds of several later generations of fishing writers: the previously mentioned, and truly extraordinary, Theodore Gordon. *The Complete Fly Fisherman,* which McDonald assembled more than thirty years after Gordon's death, revealed to readers one of the most creative and engaging minds in American fishing history, and gave American fly fishers their foremost literary hero. It should be on anyone's short list of America's finest fishing books.

Gordon, though he did not develop a formal set of fly patterns, or a formal imitation theory, or anything else, may very well have been the foremost proponent between 1890 and 1915 of the need for such things in America. He was tireless in his search for ways to adapt British ideas to specific American situations, and he tended to reject popular flies (such as the Royal Coachman) that did not plainly imitate a known insect. Through a quarter-century of notes and letters published in *Forest and Stream* and the British *Fishing Gazette*, as well as through conversations and correspondence with many fishermen, he kept dry flies on the minds of many people, and he never stopped asking interesting questions.

I like to think that Gordon represented some of the best impulses of fishermen of his day, whether British or American. He was open to new ideas, and he was always wondering about things. His reconsiderations of old theories are some of the most intriguing passages in McDonald's book.

And with Gordon and his rise as a leading spokesman for fly fishermen and their needs in America, we come to the singular publishing event that resulted in the first American books on the dry fly.

THE BOOK AND ITS COMPANIONS

This story begins, like so many episodes in sporting publishing, not in a book but in a magazine—in this case *Field and Stream*. In a six-part series of articles commencing in the June 1912 issue and entitled "The Dry Fly in America," La Branche laid out his experiences and his theories. Remember that he had cast his first dry fly only thirteen years earlier, then listen to how the editor of *Field and Stream* introduced him:

> If any man in America deserves the title The American Halford, it is without doubt Mr. George La Branche, who has been for many years the foremost champion of the dry fly in America. What Mr. La Branche has to offer is not a re-hash of the writings of Dewar, Halford and other British authors but his own practical dry fly experience on American trout streams. As we expected, following the introductory articles by E. M. Gill, there would be a general awakening of interest in the dry fly in America, and an abundant crop of transcriptions from the writings of English authorities on the subject are to be looked for in the outdoor press. But the man who writes from actual experience with the dry fly on American trout streams is *rara avis* indeed, and it is with considerable pride that we offer to our readers the following series of five articles [six were eventually published—P.S.] which comprise advance chapters from Mr. La Branche's forthcoming book on the dry fly.

This statement captures much of what we deal with when we attempt to understand fishing history. If we read only this, and La Branche's articles, we would suffer the same tunnel vision that allowed earlier generations of writers to read only Gordon's material and assume that Gordon alone was writing about the dry fly. The editor of *Field and Stream* was either unaware of all the other material on dry flies that had been published in America back into the 1880s or, as sometimes happens, did not like to acknowledge contributions made by periodicals other than his own and so didn't mention Gordon and the rest. For whatever reason, the editor happily took credit for introducing the dry fly to American readers through earlier articles by Emlyn Gill, and then pronounced La Branche as the American master on this subject.

Emlyn M. Gill, like Gordon, La Branche, and many other of the leading eastern writers of the time, was a Catskill fisherman. His series of articles, "Practical Dry-Fly Fishing for Beginners," had appeared in *Field and Stream* in 1911, and it was only a year later that he produced the first American book devoted solely to dry-fly fishing.

Like his series of articles, *Practical Dry-Fly Fishing* was for beginners. It was a bright, chatty, and quite well-informed little effort for its time. Gill had read both the British and American fishing books of the previous sixty years, and quoted liberally from many of them as well as from magazine articles. He presented himself not as an expert, but as a practical person who was trying to keep this whole business simple in the face of considerable confusion and skepticism.

Gill politely discarded the "purist" approach of only casting to rising fish, recommending systematic coverage of likely water with repeated casts. He praised the great British angler-entomologists, but, like La Branche (and unlike Gordon), saw no immediate need for the American dry-fly fisherman to learn a great deal of entomology in order to catch fish; the available British patterns would do the job most of the time.

But let's be sure we understand what Gill did and *didn't* mean. He did mean that he saw no need to learn entomology. He didn't mean that fish could be caught on any old pattern. He may not have been an enthusiast of entomology, but he was a real believer in *imitation*. Listen to him on the fundamental importance of being prepared to match the insect that the fish was eating, even if you knew nothing of the scientific identification of that insect:

> It must not be forgotten that a trout from its earliest infancy has but two principal occupations— to exercise a constant watchfulness lest it fall into the clutches of its enemies and to secure its food entirely unaided. From almost the time it is hatched the little trout fry has no one to show it what to eat; it must make its own selection of food. Must it be an entomologist to be able to do this? Who that has passed many days on the streams, and has performed autopsies on the fish, can doubt that at times, at least, the trout is most carefully selective in its food? What angler is there who has not seen in a trout's stomach the black mass made up of thousands of little gnats, all of one species, and failed to find a single specimen of another insect, though several varieties of flies, at other times greedily taken by the fish, may have been on the water at the time this fish was feeding?

Gill's little book apparently did okay. There was also a British edition in 1912, and another American edition in 1919, the year after he died. But he has been relegated to the "also-ran" category by most later writers; not so much for any great failing of his book, which was after all just an introductory primer, but because of the book that followed two years later. Arnold Gingrich, in *The Joys of Trout* (1973), summed it up fairly well:

> The luckless Gill, lacking either the matinee idol charisma of a La Branche or the elfin wispy mystery of a Gordon, has been minimized rather than magnified by the passage of time and clings today to a sort of mini-eminence, a relatively pygmy position of puny stature among the stalwarts of American angling annals.

Gingrich was right to that point, but then he went on to describe what a much longer shadow Gill might have cast if only he had done a bunch of things—like create an American angling entomology—that Gill had no desire to do anyway. It's a little like saying that Lou Gehrig could now be remembered for hitting more home runs than Babe Ruth, if only he'd hit more home runs than Babe Ruth.

But whatever Gill did or didn't do, the plot in this literary saga begins to thicken at this point. Austin Francis, in *Catskill Rivers* (1983), tells us that Gill and La Branche had some sort of falling out about this time. In his book, Gill referred to La Branche in glowing, almost adulatory tones, but apparently the relationship cooled. Both men were members of the exclusive Angler's Club of New York, from which Gill mysteriously resigned in 1912.

The plot thickens a bit more, at least in retrospect, with the appearance of the second American book on dry-fly fishing. It was not La Branche's book, but a little volume called *Fishing with Floating Flies* (1913, by Samuel Camp). Camp would spend most of his subsequent life (he died in 1952) as a full-time outdoor writer, which makes him unusual among the leaders of the dry-fly revolution, who tended more to be prosperous hobby-ists (or, as Nick Lyons puts it, "brilliant amateurs") than professional fishermen. Camp later enlarged on the subject, publishing *Taking Trout with the Dry Fly* in 1935.

What is curious about Camp, besides his book being totally neglected by the fishing writers who have attempted to chronicle American dry-fly literature, is that he did a pretty good job. His book is almost devoid of any literary quality; if Gill was practical, Camp was downright nuts-and-bolts dull. But he knew what he was talking about, and he had an appealing sense of reality. He stood back far enough, indeed he was the first of these book authors to do so, to see that every theory had its day, and that the smart fisherman was prepared to apply any of them that looked promising at any time:

> As to the basic principle of trout fly-fishing, that of approaching with the utmost fidelity, in the dressing and manipulation of the artificial fly, the shade, shape, and movement of the natural fly, various "schools" have arisen from time to time in advocacy of the greater importance of coloration as compared to size and shape (within reasonable limits, of course), or, again, of the action imparted to the artificial fly as compared with its coloration, size, or form. Into matters of this sort it is needless to enter here. The practical, common-sense point of view would seem to be that neither the proper color nor the correct imitative action of the artificial fly can be safely disregarded by the angler; moreover, the size and the shape of the artificial, varied to suit the occasion, are factors of great importance.

Camp pointed out that Americans did not tend to concern themselves with precise imitation, and agreed with Gill (though not mentioning him by name) that most of the time, a good selection of typical British patterns will cover most of the dry-fly fisherman's needs. He devoted a lot of space to explaining how to fish dry flies when trout aren't rising—how to read the water for the likely spots, how to cast over them, and so on. He included a chapter on entomology, largely quoted from the works of others. All in all, he came across as someone who had put in a good bit of time on the stream, and knew how to catch trout on dry flies. I don't yet know why the book has been so unanimously ignored by dry-fly writers; it contained at least as much information as Gill's did.

There is something else in our selective memory about these writers, something impossible to measure. It is what a historian-professor of mine once described as "the imponderable element of personality." La Branche was a widely admired man, a member of all the right upper-crust circles, not only in New York angling society but in New York financial matters. In a field of literary endeavor that has been largely chronicled by members of the socially exclusive Angler's Club of New York, that would be a huge leg up. I suspect that even if La Branche's book had not been as good as it was, it would have won the long-term competition for popularity just because generations of these club members would have praised it without hesitation in their own writings, training the next generation to reflexively do the same without even wondering if there might have been other books.

The Dry Fly and Fast Water appeared in 1914, with later editions in 1921, 1951, and 1967. You have the book in your hands now, so I will only point out a few of its strengths.

The very title announces a declaration of independence. The British streams where the dry fly reached its formal maturity in the late 1800s were generally quiet—the famous "chalk streams" of Halford, Skues, and many other wonderful writers. It is a great oversimplification to say that British streams are smooth and American streams are rough, but La Branche identified a fundamental difference in the needs of the two groups of anglers, and aimed his study at the freestone mountain streams that occupied most of the attention of his fellow fly fishermen. By doing so, he became, in the words of Vincent Marinaro, "principal architect of the early American style of fishing the rough mountain waters." (Just as Marinaro became the first important writer on the American equivalents of the British chalk streams).

I enjoy *The Dry Fly and Fast Water* most now for its writing; La Branche was an engaging and entertaining writer, who tells his little tales clearly and makes his points well. But among historians it is distinguished for its high level of new ideas, or freshly reconsidered old ideas. There are many intriguing little asides, about all manner of interesting things, that make the book consistently enjoyable. His consideration of the nymph feeding of trout and of the nature of rise forms are but two examples of these. But it is in his analysis of the imitation issue that La Branche made his place among theorists.

It wasn't, as is sometimes claimed, that he did not care about imitation. What he didn't care about, at least not a great deal, was fly pattern. He had a theory of imitation that placed other things above tying a fly to look very much like the insect. You will see that the first thing in his imitative theory was the position of the fly upon the water, followed in descending order of importance by the fly's action, its size, its form, and its color. He was what later writers would call a presentationist; if you put the fly over the fish right, you will be doing most of what needs doing.

He, more than Gill and Camp, popularized the very non-British approach of fishing the water—casting to likely spots of holding water—though none of them really originated it, most of wet-fly fishing being based on it for centuries. He also recommended repeatedly casting to such spots, or to known fish, in what he called "forcing the rise," or what has been called "creating a hatch" to which a fish will eventually rise after watching enough flies go over (though La Branche did not pretend to understand exactly what the fish made of it).

He also has been given credit for yet another separation from British ways, with his "bounce cast," by which he caused his dry fly to skip a bit as it landed (Gordon experimented with what he called "deliberate drag" as well). La Branche wasn't the first to attempt to give motion and life to a floating fly, but he did get the idea new attention. Leonard Wright and other later writers have, of course, developed manipulation of floating flies into a whole sub-pursuit of presentation.

Leonard Wright comes to mind often in discussing these early dry-fly men, because he recognized their peculiar position. They were not starting cold with unknown streams or without preexisting theories. They carried to the rivers a great deal of Old World baggage, in the form of what they had read by Halford, Dewar, and others, and their new ideas and theories grew out of that foundation. As Wright put it in *Fishing the Dry Fly as a Living Insect* (1972), a book with the same fresh spirit as *The Dry Fly and Fast Water*, "It is interesting to speculate on what American dry-fly fishing would have been like today if it had sprung up spontaneously under our conditions and on our rivers." That is, what would we have made of it if we had not set about to hybridize British theories with American needs?

Interestingly, in his second book, *The Salmon and the Dry Fly* (1924), La Branche seemed to show greater interest in the need for a realistic fly, that is a fly that is "as nearly as human hands may fashion it, an exact imitation of the natural insect." I offer that as an example of how many exceptions there are in this story. Halford himself admitted that sometimes he liked to put a cast over a likely spot, just to see if a fish would come up. These were real people, not cardboard cutouts, and they learned and changed as their lives went on.

OF GORDON, AND OTHERS

Where does all this leave Theodore Gordon, now so often hailed as the father of the American dry fly? In their books, Gill, Camp, and La Branche reveal no debt to Gordon, whose passion was for creating accurate (and beautiful) flies to imitate either specific insects or specific types of insects that he did not think British flies suited.

Well, it leaves him still a very important figure in the long run, because it was Gordon, not any of these others, who more or less launched the still-thriving Catskill "school" of fly tying. In the dynamic fly fishing culture of that region, fishermen had the good sense to adopt the best of all these innovators, and Gordon gets the lion's share of the credit for the modern Catskill fly.

But where did it leave him at the time the books were being published? That is a bit less clear. Gordon made only passing mention of Gill's book in his letters, and made no mention at all of Camp. His relationship with La Branche is more interesting.

Over the years since La Branche's book was published, as these early dry-fly writers were canonized and their works were studied and restudied, there grew a belief that La Branche and Gordon were close friends who often fished or dined together. There were some nice bits of evidence for this, including Gordon's glowing review of La Branche's book, published in *Forest and Stream*, and La Branche's even more adulatory remarks in the *Fishing Gazette* upon the death of Gordon. La Branche called Gordon "perhaps, the greatest student of fly-fishing in this country, and without exception the best fly tier I have ever known," and looked forward to sharing a place with him in the "great beyond." It was a touching

La Branche (above, left) and Edward R. Hewitt fishing in the early 1930s

COURTESY OF THE AMERICAN MUSEUM OF FLY FISHING

and powerful tribute.

But reading over the mentions of La Branche in Gordon's notes and letters, I find only one actual mention of a meeting: in June of 1914, La Branche, Edward Ringwood Hewitt, and Gordon had dinner together. What I do find is ample evidence of a warm correspondence between La Branche and Gordon, based on mutual admiration and interest in fly fishing's questions. Also in June of 1914, when Gordon reviewed La Branche's book, he said only that he knew La Branche "by reputation." Most important, later in his life, probably in the early 1950s, La Branche wrote the following, a small manuscript fragment that now resides in the La Branche Collection at the American Museum of Fly Fishing:

> Many things have been said recently in more or less permanent print about the personal relations of the late Mr. Theo. Gordon and myself. I had the pleasure of corresponding with him for many years but met him but three times, twice appointments [this word unclear—P.S.] on the river. I considered him a great friend and companion. We discussed fishing naturally—and when I told him that I was fishing a dry fly on any part of the water rather than confining my efforts to the still water of pools, or slow running currents, he told me that I was belittling [this word unclear—P.S.] the theory of dry fly fishing. He agreed with G. A. B. DeWar and Halford that what I was doing was an affectation and that the dry fly should be used on slow flowing water over rising fish only. I was upset more than a little, but persevered with my idea.

What we have here, then, was a pair of well-mannered sportsmen who disagreed about some pretty important things but enjoyed doing so. In his letter to the *Fishing*

Gazette about Gordon's death, La Branche couldn't resist a little aside about Gordon seeming to come around a little bit to La Branche's viewpoint on the importance of size and form of the fly; if only their correspondence had survived, we might have a whole new reason to admire them both for their powers of argument.

Gordon died in 1915, just a year before someone attempted to produce the angling entomology he yearned for. In 1916, Louis Rhead, a highly successful commercial artist and prolific fishing writer who had written about dry-fly fishing as early as 1908 in *Outing* magazine, produced *American Trout Stream Insects*. The frontispiece was a pencil portrait of George La Branche, another testament to his stature.

Rhead's book has been one of American fishing writing's foremost loose cannons, rolling around on the deck of fishing theory to the great annoyance of most later writers. Rhead, like Camp, Gill, and La Branche, eschewed formal entomology, but went ahead and created an elegantly involved system of imitations, all more or less original with him. In his book he identified dozens of important insects, all named by him and now more or less impossible to connect with known emergences (though I have several times said that it would be a great exercise for some knowledgeable Catskill fisherman to try to reconcile Rhead's drawings of insects with real insects found on the stream today).

Rhead's book was too big a leap, and the flies have been all but ignored for half a century. The prominent New York tackle firm of Williams Mills marketed them for some years, and they apparently did sell, but none—not a one of them, amazingly enough—made it into the permanent fly collection of American fishermen. They were, admittedly, a strange batch of things, heavily wrapped, improbably thick or colorful, but they were perhaps the single most impressive burst of originality to that point in American fly tying. They just didn't look like they would work. And who knows, today, if they did?

But Rhead was a tireless writer and self-promoter, and through the teens and twenties he produced many excellent and pioneering articles on fly fishing, including some fine work on dry flies. He showed how to fish dry flies downstream, how to imitate a wide range of insects, and much more.

Rhead is important in our story partly because he shows the growing fashionableness of dry flies and fly-tying theory after La Branche's book was published, and partly because he, too, eventually got crosswise of the La Branche reputation. Though I have not been able to track down any contemporary or published accounts of the incident, it seems that La Branche and Rhead had a run-in too. Eugene Connett, famous as the founder of the Derrydale Press and author of several very good fishing books, remembered the episode in a letter to fishing historian Austin Hogan, written in 1965 and now in the Austin Hogan Collection at the American Museum of Fly Fishing:

> Rhead was a conceited little fellow, a very delightful artist, and the worst fly designer that God ever put breath in. I once arranged a debate between him and my good friend George La Branche, when I was president of the Angler's Club of New York, on the subject of exact imitation in tying trout flies. La Branche chewed poor Rhead into small pieces and spit him out. It was quite cruel and I always felt a bit guilty about have arranged the debate. This was back about 1921.

Again, we encounter a tale of the old-boy network with no way of knowing if the debate really was that one-sided. And as I read this, I wonder if perhaps La Branche, like Gordon, might have been a nicer person in his writing than he was in real life.

LATER LA BRANCHE

After the publication of *The Salmon and the Dry Fly*, La Branche gradually switched much of his attention to saltwater fishing, especially bonefish in Florida. It was said that the death of Ambrose Monell, one of his closest salmon-fishing friends, was a reason he gave up that sport. He did not abandon trout, but it is difficult to tell from surviving information just how much fishing he did for them. We know of his visits to England, and of some trips he made to the Carlisle area to fish the Pennsylvania limestone streams, and to the famous spring creek at Castalia in Ohio, but his diaries don't give us any details, and contemporary accounts haven't surfaced yet to provide what must have been some good stories. His extensive correspondence with G. E. M. Skues suggests that he trout fished fairly often.

It has always entertained me that after writing two books that sit in the first row of important works in their respective fields, this energetic and thoughtful man essentially gave up writing about fishing for the next thirty-six years. Except for a few notes in the Angler's Club *Bulletin* and one or two other items, he didn't publish.

It was not for lack of interest in fishing; he became a passionate student not only of saltwater fishing but of Florida history, natural history, and culture. It seems a shame that he never felt moved to write the sort of small masterpiece about bonefish that he did about trout.

Joe Brooks in *Salt Water Fly Fishing* (1950) wrote an account of La Branche's first bonefish on a fly:

La Branche (right) posed with his friend and salmon fishing companion, Ambrose Monell, on the steps of "The Lodge," Monell's home in Forestburgh, New York, circa 1917.

I was lucky enough to sit in on George M. L. La Branche's first encounter with a bonefish via the fly-casting method . . . . La Branche, internationally known angler and authority on trout and Atlantic salmon, had taken many bonefish on bait, but up to this time had not presented a fly to them. We went out, with Frankee Albright guiding, to fish the banks on the Gulf side of Islamorada. The water was glassy and when Frankee poled us out on the flat, the tide was so low that there was only 6 inches of water. I knew it was going to be a very tough job to even get close to a bonefish, much less hook one.

Frankee poled as Brooks watched La Branche tie a white bucktail onto his leader, then apply a liberal dose of line dressing to the underside of the fly to float it well above the bottom of the shallows. Then Frankee spotted a tailing bonefish and cautiously approached as its caudal fin flashed in the sunlight. At one point they could see its whole back contrasted against the green of a thick clump of grass.

> At 60 feet La Branche got ready to cast. At 50 he made a couple of false casts, then shot the fly out like a bullet and stopped his rod, dropping the fly lightly 2 feet in front of the tailing fish. It spied the fly at once and literally plowed up the sand to get to it. With a quick side thrust of his rod, La Branche set the hook, and then we saw that grandest of all fishing sights, a bonefish in full flight across a flat of 6-inch water. He ran a good 400 feet and then brought out the full bag of bonefish tricks while we watched his every move in that thin water. At last he was fought to a standstill, then gradually brought to boat. I heard Frankee say, as she slipped the net under him, "Congratulations, Mr. La Branche. He'll go about 9 pounds."

George La Branche died in New York City on November 18, 1961. He lived to see extraordinary changes in fly fishing, and major new developments in dry-fly fishing, such as Jennings' *Book of Trout Flies* (1935) and Marinaro's *A Modern Dry-Fly Code* (1950) and the rising use of nylon and other synthetics. A round of acclaim followed his passing, in which he was called the Babe Ruth of fly fishing, among other things. However imprecise the metaphors, the praise was well earned. He put together one of those rare theoretical works that was both good synthesis of what was known, and original thinking about what should be done next. Vincent Marinaro, who saw La Branche apply his skills on the Letort, may have described him best:

His entire fishing life was a severe contrast with the modern, narrow, and over simplistic approach of relying on pattern alone, in which all too frequently the fishing scene reveals the fisherman frantically changing flies instead of observing the trout and exploring all the available options in the all-important matter of presentation.

THE DRY FLY
AND FAST WATER

CHAPTER I
EARLY EXPERIENCES

From my earliest boyhood I have been devoted to the fly fisher's art, having been inducted into it by my father, who was an ardent angler before me. For more than twenty years I have fished the near-by streams of New York and Pennsylvania; not a season has passed without having brought to me the pleasure of casting a fly over their waters. Each recurring year I find myself, as the season approaches, eagerly looking forward to the bright days when I can again go upon the streams. In the early days of the season, however, I am content to overhaul my gear, to dream alone, or talk with others about the active days to come; for I have never enjoyed going upon the waters so long as the air still holds chill winter's bite.

During the early years of my angling I fished my flies wet or sunk. Such was the manner universally prevailing upon our streams and the manner of my teaching. I had read about the dry fly and knew that its use was general in England, which country may justly be said to be its place of origin. That this is true may not be gainsaid, yet it seems to me remarkable that with all the reputed ingenuity of Amercians the present development of dry fly fishing for trout should be almost entirely the work of British sports-men. That the use of the dry fly on streams in this country has not been more common may be due to a pardonable disinclination upon the part of expert wet fly anglers to admit the weakness of their method under conditions as they now exist. Their method has served them well, as it did their fathers before them, and perhaps they are loath to surrender it for something new. In the earlier days trout were much more abundant in our streams, and the men who fished the streams and wrote upon the subject of fly fishing in this country may have felt that a knowledge of the habits and haunts of the fish was more essential to success in taking them than the employment of any particular method. The merits of up-stream over down-stream fishing caused some discussion among anglers, and some of these discussions found permanent place in angling literature. The discussion, however, seems always to have been confined to the question of position and seems never to have been extended to the manner of fishing the flies. Individual characteristics or experiences led some to advocate a certain manner of manipulating the dropper-fly and others to recommend the sinking of the tail-fly to a greater depth; but the flies seem always to have been manipulated upon the theory that to be effective they must be constantly in motion. It seems to have been conceded by all that the flies should be always under the control and subject to the direction of the rod, thus enabling

"The flies [were] manipulated upon the theory that to be effective they must be constantly in motion." The classic cast of two or three wet flies was a popular method on Catskill rivers before the dry fly boon in American fly fishing.

the angler to simulate living insects by twitching them over or under the surface of the water—a practice that is the exact opposite of the method of the dry fly fisher, who casts a single fly lightly upon the surface of the water and permits it to float with the current over or near the spot where he knows or believes a fish to lie.

Many expert wet fly anglers in this country have been using the floating fly for years, but most of them use it only on water where they consider it may prove more effective than the wet fly—usually upon the quiet surface of a pool or on flat, slow water. Contrary to the prevailing notion, however, the floating fly is not a whit more deadly on water of this character than the wet fly, when the latter is properly fished. The difficulty in taking trout on such water may be ascribed to two causes: (1) When the water is low and clear, or where it has little motion and the surface is unruffled, the fish is likely to perceive the activities of the angler at a greater distance than is possible in rougher water, and is thus sooner warned of his approach. (2) When the angler has been careful to conceal himself from the fish, the fly cast in the usual wet fly manner is likely to be refused because of its unnatural action, the wake made by dragging the flies across the smooth surface being sufficient at times to deter even small fish from becoming interested in it. The floating fly is far more effective than the wet, "jerky" fly, because, as no motion is imparted to it, it is more lifelike in appearance. When such a fly, properly presented, is refused such refusal may be due as much to a disinclination upon the part of the fish to feed as to his suspicion having been aroused. The wet fly fished *sunk*, with no more motion given to it than is given to the floating one (a single fly being used in each case), will prove quite as deadly as the latter on smooth water; and where many casts with the dry fly may be necessary to induce a rise, the sunk fly may appeal upon the first or second attempt, because its taking demands of the fish no particular exertion. The effort of the angler to impart a "lifelike" motion to the wet fly upon the surface will often be quite enough in itself to defeat his purpose. Such effort should never be made on clear, glassy water, for, while it may occasionally be successful, unseen fish are put down.

For many years I was one of those who firmly believed that only the smooth, slow stretches of a stream could be fished successfully with the dry fly. Experience, however, has taught me that the floater, skillfully handled, is applicable to any part of a swift stream short of a perpendicular waterfall. My unorthodox method of using it—which may be described as creating a whole family of flies instead of imitating an individual member thereof—may be characterised by some as "hammering" or "flogging," and condemned as tending to make fish shy because the leader is shown so often. My answer to this is that if the blows struck by the fly are light no harm is done. And, furthermore, if showing gut to the fish really tends to make them more wary, the sport of taking them, in my estimation, is pushed up a peg.

It is not my purpose to contend that the dry fly is more effective than the wet fly, although I do believe that, under certain conditions, the dry fly will take fish that may not be taken in any other manner. I do contend, however, that a greater fascination attends its use. All game birds are pursued with the same weapon, but the more difficult birds to kill have the greater attraction for sportsmen; and my predilection for the dry fly is based on the same principle.

My first dry fly was cast over the Junction Pool—the meeting of the waters of the Willowemoc and the Mongaup—about fifteen years ago, and the fact that I cast it at all was due more to the exigency of the occasion than to any predevised plan for attempting the feat. Every day in the late afternoon or evening I noted four or five fish rising in the pool formed by these two streams, and repeated attempts upon my part to take one of them by the old method absolutely failed me, although I put forth diligent efforts. The desire to take one of these fish became an obsession, and their constant rising to every-thing but my flies exasperated me to the point of wishing that I might bring myself to the use of dynamite.

One evening in looking through my fly book I found in one of the pockets a clipping from the *Fishing Gazette*, which I had placed there during the preceding winter. If my memory serves me, I think this article was entitled "Casting to Rising Fish." At any rate, the caption was such that it caught my eye, as it seemed to suggest the remedy for which I was searching. The article proved to be an account of the experience of an angler who used the dry fly for trout, and his exposition of the manner of using it seemed so clear that I determined to try it myself upon the pool over the rising fish in the late afternoon. Barring my inability to execute properly the things the author described and that I was called upon to do, the only stum-bling-block in my way was the impossibility of my obtain-ing an artificial fly that resembled the insects upon which the trout were feeding, and the author laid a great deal of stress upon the necessity of using such an imitation. I remember that, in a measure, I was mildly glad of this, because I felt that I would have an excuse for failure if I were unsuccessful. I "doctored" some wet flies into what I thought to be a fair imitation of the dry fly by tying the wings forward so that they stood at right angles to the body, and then sallied forth to the pool. On my way to the stream I went alternately hot and cold betwixt hope and fear. I rehearsed in my mind all the things I had to do, and I think I was coldest when I thought of having to float the fly. The writer had recommended the use of a paraffin-oil as an aid to buoyancy, and this commodity was about as easily procurable in Sullivan County at that time as the philosopher's stone; in my then frame of mind the latter would probably have proven quite as good a buoyant. The pool was but a stone's throw from the house, and I arrived there in a few minutes, only to find a boy disturbing the water by dredging it with a worm. Him I lured away with a cake of chocolate, sat down to wait for the rise which came on shortly, and by the time I was ready there were a half dozen good fish feeding on the surface. I observed two or three sorts of flies about and on the water, to none of which my poor, mussed-up Queen-of-the-Waters bore the slightest resemblance. This did not deter me, however, and I waded boldly out to a position some forty feet below and to the right of the pool. My first cast amazed me. The fly alighted as gently as a natural insect upon the surface, and, watching it as it floated down toward the spot where a fish had been rising, I saw it disappear, a little bubble being left in its place. Instinctively I struck, and to my astonishment found that I was fast in a solid fish that leaped clear of the water. The leaping of this fish was a new experience, as I had never seen a trout jump as cleanly from the water. After a few flights and a determined rush or two I netted him—a rainbow trout just over a foot long and the first I had ever taken. This variety of trout had been placed in the stream a few years before as an experiment, and few had been caught. Stowing my prize in my creel, I prepared for another attempt as soon as the excitement in the pool had subsided. The fly I had used was bedraggled and slimy and would not float, so I knotted on another. My second attempt was as successful as the first, and I finally netted, after a tussle, a beautiful native trout that weighed a little over one pound. Four fine fish fell to my rod that evening, all within half an hour, and the fly

La Branche cast a dry fly for the first time on the famous Junction Pool where the Willowemoc and the Mongaup join to form the Beaverkill River.

PHOTO BY MATTHEW VINCIGUERRA, COURTESY OF JUDIE DARBEE VINCIGUERRA

was taken on the first cast each time. If such had not been the case I doubt very much if I should have succeeded, because I am certain that my confidence in the method would have been much weakened had I failed to take the first fish, and my subsequent attempts might not have been made at all, or, if made, would probably have ended in failure.

For several years after my first experience with the floating fly I used it in conjunction with the wet fly, and until I read Mr. Halford's "Dry Fly Fishing," when, recognising his great authority and feeling that the last word had been said upon the subject, I used the dry fly only on such water as I felt he would approve of and fished only rising fish. Some time later on I read George A. B. Dewar's "Book of the Dry Fly." Mr. Dewar says: "I shall endeavour to prove in the course of this volume that the dry fly is never an

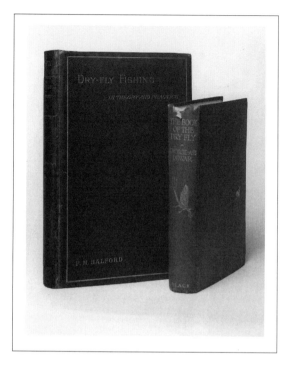

Two English books, Halford's Dry Fly Fishing in Theory and Practice *and Dewar's* Book of the Dry Fly, *served as La Branche's early sources of dry-fly knowledge.*

COURTESY OF THE AMERICAN MUSEUM OF FLY FISHING

affectation, save when resorted to in the case of brawling, impetuous streams of mountainous districts, where it is practically impossible of application." Here again I felt inclined to listen to the voice of authority and felt that I must abandon the dry fly. I was accustomed to fish such streams as the Beaverkill, Neversink, Willowemoc, and Esopus, in New York; the Brodhead and Shohola, in Pennsylvania; the Saco and its tributaries, in New Hampshire, and others of similar character—all brawling, impetuous, tumbling streams—and it seemed to me that by continuing to use the dry fly on them I was profaning the creed of authority and inviting the wrath of his gods upon my head. Since then, however, I have continued the use of the dry fly on all of these streams, and a number of years ago abandoned the use of the wet fly for all time.

Since I began casting the fly over the streams of the

region I have mentioned their character has greatly changed in many particulars, and conditions are not the same as they were twenty years ago. The natural streams themselves have changed; the condition of the water flowing in them has changed; the sorts of fish inhabiting the waters have changed; and the methods of taking the fish have changed, or should change; and it is to show why this last is true that the following pages are written.

The changes that have taken place in the character of our mountain streams may be attributed to many causes, chief of which, however, is the destruction of the timber which at one time covered the hills through which they have their course. During the frequent and long-continued droughts the denuded hills, baked hard as rock, shed the occasional summer showers as readily as the back of the proverbial duck; the streams become turbid torrents for a few hours, after which they run down, seemingly to a lower mark than before. So long as the forests covered the watersheds the rains as they fell were soaked up by the loose and porous earth about the roots of the trees, were cooled in the shade of the leaves and branches, and slowly percolated into the tiny brooklets through which they were fed to the streams for many days. Under present conditions the temperature of the streams is much higher than formerly, and, while the temperature has seldom risen to a point where it has been fatal to the fish, it has risen in many streams to a point that is distasteful to the native brook-trout (*Salvelinus fontinalis*).

It is not unreasonable to assume that the heat of the water has a very deleterious effect upon the vitality of the fish during certain years when the droughts are long sustained and, should the condition have existed for a great length of time prior to the spawning season, that the progeny for the year would probably come into being lacking the vitality necessary to overcome the attacks of natural enemies and disease. A bad spawning season, of course, reduces the hatch for the year, but is ordinarily not noticed by the angler until two or three years later, at which time the unusually small number of immature fish taken becomes a matter of comment among the frequenters of the streams. A native angler who has made it a practice to visit the spawning-grounds of trout for over twenty-five years stated to me that during the season of 1910 the redds were occupied by trout, but that not a fish spawned on any of them in a stretch of nearly a mile of the stream which flows past his home and which was under his constant observation during the entire season. It is difficult for me to believe that such a thing could have been possible, yet I know the man to be a careful and accurate observer, and his statement must be given credence. He seemed frightened at the prospect and alarmed as to the future of the stream, and he besought me for an explanation of the condition—which I was unable to give. My diary for that year had been destroyed, so that I was then, and am now, unable to even theorise as to whether or not the failure to spawn was due to weather conditions prevailing at that time. Let us hope, assuming that my informant was not mistaken, that the curious condition observed by him was confined to the stretch of the stream that he investigated. Let us hope, further, that the fish, even in that stream, will not become addicted to such an ungenerous and unnatural habit.

Great numbers of trout must be destroyed in the periodical freshets that carry masses of ice tearing and grinding over the beds of the mountain streams. When the ice breaks up gradually there is very little danger to the fish; but a sudden and continued thaw, accompanied by a steady fall of warm rain, washes the snow from the hillsides, swells the streams into wild torrents, and rips the very bottom out of them. Any one who has witnessed the forming of an ice-jam and its final breaking must marvel at the possibility of any fish or other living thing in its path escaping destruction, so tremendous is the upheaval. A few years ago a jam and freshet on the Brodhead, besides uprooting great trees along the banks, lifted three iron bridges within as many miles from their stone abutments and carried each of them a hundred yards down-stream, leaving them, finally, mere masses of twisted iron. These bridges were twelve or fifteen feet above the normal flow of the stream, yet, even so, they did not escape destruction. How, then, is it possible for stream life to stand against such catastrophe? Furthermore, this scouring of the beds of the streams by ice and debris carried down during the floods undoubtedly destroys great quantities of the larvae of the aquatic insects which form an important part of the trout's food, and this, too, indirectly affects the supply of fish available to the angler's rod. After a severe winter and a torrential spring there is a noticeable dearth of fly upon the water—another of the many causes of lament of the fly fisherman of to-day.

Directly or indirectly, all of the conditions above described are the result of the ruthless cutting of the timber from the hills. Happily, there is reason to hope that these conditions are not going to grow worse, because the present movement toward the preservation of the forests seems to be gaining headway; conservation of nature's resources will come to be a fixed policy of our National and State Governments, and if the policy is pushed with vigour and persistence our children's children may some day see our old familiar streams again singing gaily through great woods like those our fathers knew.

With the elements, man, beast, and bird all intent upon its destruction, it is a marvel that our native brook-trout survives. But live on he does, though his numbers constantly decrease. The great gaps left in his ranks are being filled by the alien brown trout—his equal in every respect but that of beauty. True, there is a wide difference of opinion in this particular, and there are some who will go so far as to say that the brown trout is, all round, the better fish for the angler. When feeding he takes the fly quite as freely as the native trout, leaps vigorously when hooked, grows rapidly to a large size, and seems better able to withstand abnormal changes in the temperature of the water, which are so often fatal to *fontinalis*. No one deplores the scarcity of our own beautiful fish more than I do; but we must not be blind to the facts that the brown trout is a game-fish, that he is in our streams and there to stay, and that our streams are suited to him. He is a fish of moods and often seems less willing to feed than the native trout; but for that reason alone, if for no other, I would consider him the sportier fish. When both varieties are taking freely and their fighting qualities compared, it is not easy to decide which is the gamer. The leaping of the brown trout is often more impressive than the determined resistance of the native trout, and the taking of a particularly active or particularly sluggish fish of either variety is frequently made the basis for an opinion. It seems to me that, in any event, the taking of even a single fair fish of either variety on the fly is an achievement to be put down as a distinct credit to the angler's skill and something to be proud of and to remember. Our native brook-trout is much loved of man. It has come to be something more than a fish: it is an ideal. It will always hold first place in the hearts of many anglers. I fear, however, that it must yield first place in the streams to its European contemporary, he having been endowed by nature with a constitution fitted to contend against existing conditions and survive.

My many years' experience upon the streams of New York and Pennsylvania have brought me to realise that changed conditions call for an expertness of skill and knowledge that anglers of the past generation did very well without. The streams now are smaller, the fish in them fewer and warier, and the difficulties of the angler who would take them greater. Three flies fished down-stream may still be a permissible method for those who pursue the trout of the wilderness, but the sportsman should now be willing to adopt the use of the single light surface fly when pursuing the trout of our domestic waters; and, if he does adopt it, as he gains in skill he will come at last to realise that it has a virtue not possessed by its wet brother. I can illustrate my point best by quoting an experience of my own that happened several years ago.

One day, while fishing an up-State stream, I met a dear old clergyman, who, after watching me for a long time, came up and said: "Young man, I have fished this stream for nearly forty years, and they will tell you at the house that I have been accounted as good as any man who ever fished here with a fly. I have killed some fine fish, too; but in all that time I have never been able to take trout as regularly as you have taken them in the few days you have been here. I am told that you use the dry fly and have some particular patterns. If it is not asking too much, will you be good enough to give me their names and tell me where they may be obtained?" I gave him the information he asked, and volunteered some instruction by pointing out that his gear was not suitable for the work, convincing him that such was the case by placing my own rod in his hands. We sat in the shade for a couple of hours exchanging ideas, and to prove or explode a theory of mine he agreed to fish a certain pool with me later in the day. He used my rod and rose and killed a brown trout of one pound five ounces, a little later leaving the fly in a heavier fish. He was an expert at placing the fly, but, not being used to the stiffer rod and lighter gut, he struck too hard, with the resultant smash. Being a good angler, he easily overcame this difficulty. He now fishes only with a rod of fine action and power, which enables him to place his fly easily, delicately, and accurately a greater distance that was possible with the "weeping" rod he formerly used. This he abandoned once and for all, and with it the wet fly. He came into the knowledge and enjoyment of the dry fly method, and he has since then frankly admitted to me that he greatly regretted having realised so late in life that the actual taking of trout constitutes but a very small part of the joy of fly fishing.

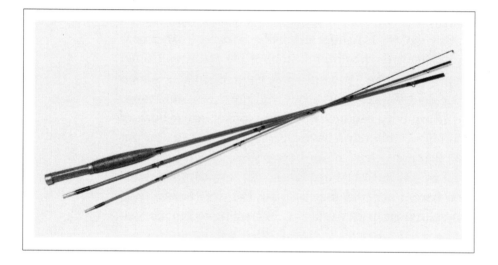

La Branche recommended "a rod of fine action and power." One of his own was the eight-foot bamboo Leonard Tournament 50DF shown above.

Pictured right is La Branche's Daisy fly box with a salmon fly in the open compartment.

<small>BOTH COURTESY OF THE AMERICAN MUSEUM OF FLY FISHING</small>

CHAPTER II
THE VALUE OF OBSERVATION

Several years ago I was looking on at a tennis match between the champion of America and one of the best men England ever sent to this country, and as I watched their play I could not help but marvel at the accuracy with which the players placed their shots. Their drives were wonderful for direction and speed. On nearly every return the ball barely cleared the net and was seldom more than a few inches above the top as it passed over. A friend who knew many of the experts told me how they attained to their remarkable precision. It was the custom of many of them, he said, when preparing for the big matches, to practise for accuracy by driving the ball against a wall. He said this was particularly true of the American champion, and that it was not unusual for him to use up a dozen or more balls in a day's practice. The wall had painted across its face a line of contrasting colour at a height from the ground equivalent to that of the top of a regulation tennis net, and upon the line were painted a number of disks about ten inches in diameter. Standing at a distance from the wall equivalent to the distance of the base-line of a regulation tennis-court from the net, the player would return the ball on its rebound from the wall, striving each time to so place it that it would strike just above the line. The accomplishment of a satisfactory score after a succession of the drives would convince the player that he had good control of his stoke, and he would then turn his attention to the disks, against each of which he would drive twenty or more shots, taking them in turn and keeping a record of hits in each case. The accuracy developed by such practice was truly remarkable, and I hesitate to mention the number of times in succession one expert made clean hits—it seemed an incredible number.

I have seen golfers practising the weak places in their game for hours with as much zeal and earnestness as if they were playing a match, and a polo player of my acquaintance practises his strokes upon a field at his home, riding his ponies as daringly and recklessly as though a championship depended on his efforts. The devotees of these and similar active sports are keenly alive to the necessity of constant practice, that spirit of competition which is so much a part of them making any endeavour that will aid toward high efficiency, or improve game or form, seem worth while. And in all sports, particularly those in which the competition is individual, whenever and wherever opportunity presents itself there will be found hundreds of enthusiasts following every play of the expert, keenly studying his method, observing his form, and absorbing and storing the knowledge so gained for their own practice later on court or field. So, too, even though competition has no place in fly fishing, and should have none, the angler ought to strive always to "play a good game." He should practise the tactics of his art with the same zeal as do the followers of competitive sports if he hopes ever to become an expert fly fisherman in the highest sense of that much misused term.

The casual angler who looks upon fishing as merely

incidental to his periods of recreation, during which his chief concern is the recuperation of tired brain and unstrung nerves, may feel that he is making a business of his pleasure by devoting much time to the study of his angling. In a measure, this is true, and it would be asking much, indeed, of him who thinks of fly fishing only as a pastime. But to him who realises that it is a sport—a sport that is also an art—there is no incident, complex or simple, that is unworthy of his attention and consideration. No sport affords a greater field for observation and study than fly fishing, and it is the close attention paid to the minor happenings upon the stream that marks the finished angler. The careless angler frequently overlooks incidents, or looks upon them as merely trivial, from which he might learn much if he would but realise their meaning at the time.

Of greatest importance to the dry fly angler is that mastery of the rod and line that enables him to place his fly lightly and accurately upon the water. I venture to assert that one who has had the advantage of expert instruction in handling a rod, and is thereby qualified to deliver a fly properly, will raise more trout upon his first attempt at fishing a stream than another who, though he knows thoroughly the haunts and habits of the fish, casts indifferently. The contrast between the instructed novice and the uninstructed veteran would be particularly noticeable were they to cast together over the same water in which fish were rising freely. Whether or not the novice would take more fish than the veteran is another question. Lacking experience, the novice would probably hook few fish and land fewer. But he would be starting right, and the necessity of overcoming later on that bad form likely to be acquired by all who begin without competent instruction would be eliminated, and the stream knowledge of the veteran would come to him in time.

La Branche demonstrates casting in Central Park
Courtesy O. T. Gidstad

The beginner should watch the expert at work and should study particularly the action of the rod. He should note that the power which impels the line forward starts from the butt, travels the entire length of the rod, is applied by a slight forward push rather than by a long sweep, and ends in a distinct snap. He will soon learn that the wrist must do the real work, and no better scheme for teaching this has ever been devised than the time-honoured one of holding a fly book or a stone between the casting arm and the body. The proper action of the rod will be best learned if he fasten that part of the butt below the reel to the forearm with a piece of string, a strap of leather, or a stout rubber band, the effect of which device will be to stop the rod in an almost perpendicular position when the line is retrieved. The pull of the line as it straightens out behind him will be distinctly felt, will give him a good idea of the power and action of his rod, and serve as a signal for the forward cast. He should practise casting as often as his spare time will allow—over water when possible, but over grass if necessary. He should not wait until the stream is reached and actual fishing problems begin to press upon his notice for solution. His mind will then be occupied with many other things; hence, the knack of handling the rod should have been already acquired.

After the beginner is satisfied that he can properly place and deliver his fly he should turn his attention to the study of the fish and the currents of the stream. If he has been a wet fly angler his experiences will stand him in good stead, as it will qualify him to locate the likely haunts of the fish. Long and varied though his experience may have been, however, the use of the dry fly will open avenues of observation and knowledge that were hidden from him while he practised the old method. My own experience is responsible for this rather broad statement, but not until after I had become an ardent advocate of the dry fly, and had abandoned the wet fly for good and all, did I realise the truth of it. In the beginning I was ever on the alert for rising fish, and, instead of boldly assailing promising water, wasted much time, on many occasions, scrutinising the water for some indication that a fish was feeding. In this way I frequently discovered non-feeding fish lying in places where I had not expected to find them. Such fish were then the more easily approached because I was able to assume a position myself that would not disclose my presence. Just as frequently, too, I have seen fine fish cruising about, and have taken many that might have been driven away by the slightest movement on my part. In many cases I have been compelled to remain absolutely motionless for ten or fifteen minutes before a fish would come to rest long enough to make worth while an attempt to get a fly to it. Nearly every time, too, that a fish has been hooked I have seen it actually take the fly—an action always instructive, because fish vary greatly in their manner of taking, and interesting, because in it lies one of the real charms of fly fishing.

The continued use of a floating fly upon water where the angler sees no indication of feeding fish, but where experience tells him that they may lie, seems to develop in him a remarkable keenness of vision. This is a direct result, perhaps, of the attention which he gives to his fly. My own experience is that while I am watching my fly float down-stream some stone of irregular formation, peculiar colour, or difference in size from others about it, lying upon the bottom, arrests my eye, with the effect of making the water appear shallower or clearer than it really is. My fly appears to be the centre of a small area upon the surface of the water through which everything is seen as clearly as through a water-glass, the shadow of the fly itself upon the bottom often being plainly discernible. Anglers who fish the dry fly learn to identify the living shadow that appears suddenly under the fly as a trout ready to take it on its next drift down-stream, and to recognise a fish as it sidles out from the bank or swings uncertainly toward the fly just as it passes the boulder that shelters him. In either case an interesting opportunity is afforded, particularly for exercising a very necessary attribute—self-control.

It may be that many happenings I now see upon the stream passed unnoticed when I used the wet fly because of some lack of concentration and observation. If this be so, I have the newer method to thank for the development of those faculties. I have learned not to overlook a single minor happening. Perhaps my keenness to ascribe some meaning to the slightest incident has resulted in the building of many very fine structures of theory and dogma upon poor foundations. This may be true, but I am certain that their weaknesses have always become apparent to me in time; and, on the other hand, I am just as certain that I have been greatly benefited by my habit of close attention to the little things that happen on the stream. For instance, I cherished the belief for many years that one advantage of up-stream fishing lay in the fact that when the fly was taken the hook was driven into the fish's mouth instead of being pulled away, as in down-stream fishing. I thought this to be one of the strongest arguments in favour of up-stream fishing, and theoretically, it is. But I know now that many fish that take a floating fly do so when they are headed down-stream. While there are still many reasons why up-stream fishing is the better method, this particular argument no longer has weight with me.

As I remember it, the strongest admonition of my early schooling on the stream was never to remain long in one place. I was taught to believe that if a rise was not effected on the first few casts subsequent effort on that water was wasted—that the trout would take the fly at once or not at all. I clung to this belief for years, until one day I saw a fine fish lying in shallow water and took him after casting a dozen or more times. Since then I have taken fish after upward of fifty casts, and I rarely abandon an attempt for one that I can see if I feel certain that it has not discovered me. Even when I have not actually seen a fish, but have known or believed one to be lying near by, the practice has proven effective. Thus I have had the satisfaction of accomplishing a thing once believed to be impossible; but I have gained more than that: I have learned to be persevering and, what is still more important, deliberate. The man who hurries through a trout stream defeats himself. Not only does he take few fish but he has no time for observation, and his experience is likely to be of little value to him.

The beginner must learn to look with eyes that see. Occurrences of apparently little importance at the moment may, after consideration, assume proportions of great value. The taking of an insect, for instance, may mean nothing more than a rising trout; but the position occupied by this fish may indicate the position taken by others in similar water. The flash of a trout, changing his position preparatory to investigating the angler's fly, will frequently disclose the spot occupied by him before he changed his position; and, later on, when the fish are not in the keenest mood for feeding, a fly presented there accurately may bring a rise. The quick dart up-stream of a small trout from the tail of a pool is a pretty fair indication that a large fish occupies the deeper water above; it indicates just as certainly, however, that the angler has little chance of taking him, the excitement of the smaller fish having probably been communicated to his big relative.

The backwater formed by a swift current on the up-stream side of a boulder is a favourite lurking-place of brown trout. I was fishing such places one day, and found the trout occupying them in rather a taking mood. In approaching a boulder which looked particularly inviting, and while preparing to deliver my fly, I was amazed to see the tail and half the body of a fine trout out of the water at the side of the rock. For a moment I could not believe that I had seen a fish—the movement was so deliberate—and I came to the conclusion that it was fancy or that a water-snake, gliding across the stream, had shown itself. Almost immediately, however, I saw the flash of a trout as he left the backwater and dashed pell-mell into the swift water at the side of the boulder. Down-stream he came until he was eight or ten feet below the rock, when, turning sharply and rising to the surface, he took from it some insect that I could not see. Up-stream again he went, and shortly resumed his position in the dead water, showing half his body as he stemmed the current at the side of the rock. Once more this performance was repeated, and I knew I had stumbled upon an interesting experience. Hastily measuring the distance, hoping to get my fly to him before some natural insect might excite him to give another exhibition of gymnastic feeding, I dropped it about three feet above him, and, contrary to my usual method of retrieving it as it floated past the up-stream side of the boulder, I permitted it to come down riding the top of the wave, when the same flash came as the trout dashed after it. The fish could be plainly seen almost directly under the fly. As it reached the rapidly flattening water below the rock, he turned and took it viciously, immediately darting up-stream again. He was soundly hooked, however, and I netted a fine fish lacking one ounce of being a pound and a half. My experience heretofore had been that if a fly were placed a yard or so above this point and allowed to float down to the rock a feeding fish would rush forward—often as much as two feet—and take it, immediately turning or backing into his position again. I had assumed from this observation that when the fly passed the rock or backwater without a rise it should be retrieved and another try made. This fish satisfied me, however, that when really feeding, or when inclined to feed, trout may be lured comparatively long distances by inviting looking morsels. Either he did not decide to take the fly until

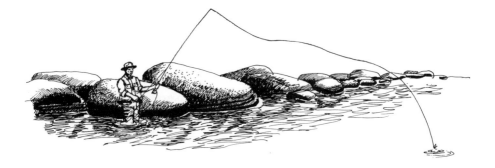

"The [bounce cast] is made with a very short line—never over twenty-five feet—and the fly alone touches the water."

just as it was passing him or else he liked the exercise of the chase. In any event, he was not peculiar in his habit, because four more fish were taken in the same manner the same day.

In most cases when the fly is cast above a boulder lying in swift water (which I consider, under certain conditions, one of the best places to look for brown trout) it will be taken as it approaches the rock, the trout darting out and retiring immediately to avoid being caught in the swifter water on either side of his stronghold. But if it is not taken, and is permitted to float down with the current, it may bring a response.

It was a somewhat similar observation which prompted the practice and, I must say, rather dubious development of what some of my friends are pleased to call the "fluttering" or "bounce" cast. This cast is supposed to represent the action of the fluttering insect, the fly merely alighting upon the water, rising, alighting again, repeating the movement three or four times at most; finally coming to rest and being allowed to float down-stream. It rarely comes off, but when it does it is deadly; and, for the good of the sport, I am glad that it is difficult, though sorry, too, for the pleasure of accomplishing it successfully is really greater than that of taking fish with it. The cast is made with a very short line—never over twenty-five feet—and the fly alone touches the water. The action of the fly is very similar to that produced by the method known as "dapping," but instead of being merely dangled from the rod, as is the case when "dapping," the fly is actually cast. It should be permitted to float as far as it will after its fluttering or skipping has ceased. The beginner practising the cast will do well to cast at right angles to the current, and he should choose rather fast water for his experimenting. The speed of the water will cause the fly to jump, and the action it should have will be the more readily simulated than if the first attempts are made on slow water.

I had made a flying trip to the Brodhead, and, with that strange fatality which seems so often to attend the unfortunate angler rushing off for a week-end in the early season, found the stream abnormally high and horrible weather prevailing. After many attempts to get into the stream, with results equally disastrous to my clothing and temper, I abandoned all idea of wading and walked and crawled along the bank, casting my fly wherever I could but rarely finding good water that could be reached, and rising but a few small fish. As there was a gale blowing in my face directly downstream, it was practically impossible to place a fly where I wished with any delicacy, and I decided to abandon the sport after trying a pool just above me that I knew contained big fish. My first cast on this water, made during a lull, fell lightly, but brought no response, and after a further half dozen fruitless attempts I began to think of the fine log fire at the house. I made one more cast, however, this time in the teeth of the wind. Using but twenty-five feet of line and a short leader, I was able to straighten both in the air. The wind kept all suspended for an instant, the fly, accompanied by a small part of the leader, finally falling upon the water, where it remained but a fraction of a second, the wind whisking it off and laying it down a foot away. This happened five or six times as the fly came down-stream, and during the time it was travelling a distance of not over eight or ten feet five trout, each apparently over a pound in weight, rose to it, but missed because it was plucked away by the wind just in time to save them. I did not get one of them, and, as it was practically impossible to continue casting under the prevailing conditions, I left the stream. It was brought home solidly to me that day, however, that it was the *action* of the fly alone that moved the fish—and my day was not badly spent. I cannot say as much of the many other days since then that I have spent in what I feel were rather foolish attempts to imitate the effect produced by the wind on that day.

The study of the positions taken by big fish when they are feeding, and those which they occupy when they are not, is an important part of the education of the fly fisher. Each time the angler takes a good fish or sees one feeding, if he will note in his diary its position, the condition of the water, temperature, atmosphere, time of day, and the insect being taken, he will soon have an accumulation of data from which he may learn how to plan a campaign against particular fish at other times. Extremely interesting in itself, the study of insects is of great value to the angler in his attempts at imitation, and the information gleaned from autopsy might not be acquired in any other manner.

It may be said to be an axiom of the fly fisher that where a small trout is seen feeding rarely need a large one be looked for. But the actions of a small fish in sight may sometimes indicate the presence of a larger one unseen. The taking of a fine trout on a certain stream in Sullivan County, on August 27, 1906, after one of those long periods of drought so common in recent years, convinced me of this. I had been waiting for even a slight fall of rain, and, quite a heavy shower having come up the evening before, I started for this stream. Upon my arrival there I was surprised to learn that not a drop of rain had fallen in weeks, and that the shower which had been heavy twenty miles away had not reached the vicinity. While driving from the station to the house at which I was to stop, along a road that paralleled the stream, the many glimpses I had of the latter filled me with misgivings. At one point the stream and road are very near each other, and, stopping my driver, I got out to look at a famous pool below a dam which had long outlived its usefulness. It was a sizzling-hot day, and at that time—eleven o'clock—the sun was almost directly overhead; yet in the crystal-clear water of this pool, with not a particle of shade to cover him, lay a native trout fourteen inches in length which afterward proved to weigh one pound three ounces. Too fine a fish, I thought, as I clambered back into the carriage, to be occupying such a place in broad daylight, and I promised myself to try for him later in the afternoon. Returning about six o'clock, I found him in the same position, and during the full twenty minutes I watched him, while he appeared to be nervously alert, he never moved. Notwithstanding the fact that everything was against me, and knowing that the chances were more than even that the fish would see me, my rod, or my line, I made my plans for approaching him; yet, busy as I was, I could not rid my mind of this ever-recurring thought: with all the known aversion of his kind to heat, and their love of dark nooks, why was this fish out in this place on such a day? Why did he not find a place under the cool shade of the dam? With the instinct strong within him to protect himself by hiding, the impulse must have been much stronger that forced him to take so conspicuous a stand—a mark to the animals which prey upon his kind. As there were absolutely no insects upon the water, and scarcely enough current to bring food of other sort to him, he could not have been feeding. The only reason, then, to account for his being there—the thought struck me forcibly enough—was his fear of a bigger fish. The logical conclusion was that if a fish of his inches (no mean adversary) exposed himself so recklessly the one that bullied him must be quite solid. I tested this fellow's appetite with a small, pinkish-bodied fly of my own invention, and, standing about forty feet below and considerably to the left, dropped it three or four feet above him; but, although it was certain he could see the fly, he made no attempt to go forward and take it. As it neared him, however, he rushed excitedly to the right and then to the left, taking the fly as it came directly over him, and, before I could realise what had happened, came down-stream toward me at a great rate. As he was securely hooked, I kept him coming, and netted him quietly at the lip of the pool.

That this fish did not take the fly the instant it fell meant to me that he was afraid to go forward into the deeper water which harboured his larger fellow; and his action as the fly appeared over him meant that, while he wanted it badly enough, he would not risk an altercation with the other, which might also have seen it. When he did finally decide that the coast was clear, he took it quickly and rushed down toward the shallower water where he might be secure against sudden attack.

If some of the theories developed in those few

moments appear fanciful, it must be remembered that my mind was occupied with the thought that the pool contained a larger fish, and the conclusions based upon the subsequent actions of this smaller one only tended to strengthen this belief. Fanciful or not, I was rewarded a few minutes later by the sight of a monster tail breaking the surface just under the water that trickled over the apron of the dam. Having prepared a gossamer leader, preferring to risk a smash to not getting a rise, I dropped a small Silver Sedge—which I used because it could be more plainly kept in sight—almost immediately in the swirl and was at once fast in a lusty fish. After many abortive attempts to lead him into the diminutive net I had with me, I flung the thing, in disgust, into the woods. I finally beached the fish and lifted him out in my hand. He was a fine brown trout, eighteen and three quarter inches in length, and weighed, the next morning, two pounds nine ounces.

While I was engaged with this fish another rose in practically the same spot under the apron of the dam. Hurriedly replacing the bedraggled fly with a new one, I waited for the trout to show himself, which he did presently, and again I was fast—this time in one of the best fish I have ever seen in these waters. It seemed an interminable length of time, though probably not over ten minutes, that I was engaged with this one, and it was impossible to move him; he kept alternately boring in toward the dam and sulking. In one of the latter fits I urged him toward me somewhat too strongly, and he was off. Immediately I was afforded a sight of what I had lost as he leaped clear of the water in an evident endeavour to dislodge the thing that had fastened to his jaw. The smash made as he struck the water still resounds in my ear, and when I say that this fish would have gone close to five pounds I but exercise the right to that license accorded all anglers who attempt to describe the size of the big ones that get away. Having one good fish in my creel, however, I really had some basis for my calculation—at any rate, he was one of the best fish I have ever risen. Examining my leader, I found it had not broken, but the telltale curl at the end proved that, in the fast-gathering gloom, I had been careless in knotting on the fly.

CHAPTER III
THE RISE

Any disturbance of the surface made by a trout is usually referred to as a "rise," but the characterisation is erroneous except where it is applied to fish feeding upon the surface. Rising fish are the delight of the dry fly fisher, but are really the easiest fish to take—provided, always, that no error is made in the presentation of the fly. The angler is called upon to exhibit a fine skill in casting, a knowledge of the insect upon which the fish is feeding, and to make the proper selection of an imitation; but he is aided materially by being apprised of the location of the fish, and is further helped by the knoweldge that he is throwing to a willing one.

The study of the habits of rising fish, or, to use a more inclusive term, feeding fish—because a feeding fish may not be a rising one—is of the utmost importance to the dry fly enthusiast, who knows how difficult it is to induce a fish feeding on or near the bottom to rise to his floater.

Inasmuch as the principal literature available on this delightful branch of angling is the work of Englishmen who have, with unfailing unanimity, used the same terms in describing the positions and actions of feeding fish, it would be unwise to attempt to employ others, and for that reason I have made use of them throughout this chapter.

Compared with our swift-flowing water, the gentle, slow-moving, chalk streams of Southern England offer greater advantages to students of the habits of feeding fish, not only because of the greater deliberation with which the trout secures his food in them but also because a greater number of aquatic insects contribute to his sustenance there than are found on our swift streams; consequently, the English student has far greater opportunity for observation. The water-weeds grow so heavily on these English streams that at times it is found necessary to cut them out to some extent if fly fishing is to be pursued. These weeds harbour great numbers of snails, shrimps, larvae, etc., of which the trout are inordinately fond, and when the fish are seeking this luscious fare the trials of the angler fishing with a floating fly are, indeed, many. Trout feeding in this manner are described as "tailing" fish, from the fact that the tail of the fish is observed breaking the surface of the water violently or

"Fish so feeding do break the surface with their tails, and, even though the tail be not actually seen, the action of this fin in maintaining the fish's equilibrium causes a swirl which is often mistaken for a rise."

gently, as the case may demand, in his efforts to secure or dislodge his prey. Heavy weed growth being unusual on our swift streams, the trout do not have the same opportunity to feed in the manner described as their English cousins, and, consequently, the American fly fisherman is not particularly interested in tailing fish; but it must not be forgotten that caddis larvae abound in our waters, and that trout occasionally pick up crawfish, snails, and other *Crustacea* and *Mollusca* from the bottom, usually in the less rapid parts of the stream. Fish so feeding do break the surface with their tails, and, even though the tail be not actually seen, the action of this fin in maintaining the fish's equilibrium causes a swirl which is often mistaken for a rise. A trout often shows his tail in rapid water but this is occasioned by the necessity of forcing his head down to overcome the force of the current after he has taken food of some sort upon the surface or just below it, and the action must not be confused with that of a fish feeding upon the bottom in the more quiet stretches.

The term "bulging" is applied to fish that are feeding below the surface upon the nymphae of insects about to undergo the metamorphosis which produces the winged fly. The trout is a very busy fellow at this time, and covers left, centre, and right field with equal facility; but he occasionally misses, and at the instant of his viciously breaking the surface of the water the insect may be seen taking its laboured flight—escaping by a hair's breadth the death which pursued it. When trout are feeding in this manner the angler's patience is taxed to the utmost, and after a succession of flies has been tried without success the discomfited angler may be excused if he concludes that his artificial is not a good imitation. He may not be far wrong.

Although aside from the main subject of dry fly fishing, I will in this connection attempt to show how the

"The term 'bulging' is applied to fish that are feeding below the surface upon the nymphae of insects about to undergo the metamorphosis which produces the winged fly."

sunk fly may be used successfully against the "bulger." As the nymph is still enclosed in its shuck, or case, it is quite obvious that an artificial fly made with wings is not an imitation of it. Consequently, a hackle-fly should be used even though it, too, is a poor imitation. A suggestion of the general hue of the natural is quite sufficient. The cast is made some distance above the feeding fish, so that the fly will approach the trout approximately as the nymph would, *i.e.*, under water and rising. If no attempt be made to impart motion the fly drifting with the current will be more natural in its action than the angler can hope to make it appear by manipulation. Besides, the trout is an excellent judge of pace, and, making for a natural-looking morsel, is sorely disappointed and not likely to come again if it is jerked away from him at the moment he is about to take it. One fly only should be used, and quite as much care is required in its delivery as would be necessary were a floating fly being presented. Errors made in casting are more readily concealed by the current in the case of the sunk fly.

When the attention of the fish is fixed upon insects beneath the surface it is difficult to attract his notice to a floating fly, except, perhaps, at such times as the fly appears before him when he is close to the surface; but it can be done—and in two ways. Fish so feeding are moving about, darting here and there taking nymphae. A swirl made by the fish in all likelihood only marks the place where he was, and he may be a yard or more upstream, or to right or left, where he went to secure the nymph. If the swirl is made by his tail at the time he starts for the insect and not at the moment he takes it, there is little knowledge as to his actual position to be gained from the disturbance; the only indication is that he is feeding. The angler must be able to distinguish between the disturbance made by a bulger feeding under water and that made by a fish taking a winged insect upon the surface—often not a very difficult thing to do— and he must conduct his campaign accordingly. The signs of the surface-feeding fish are easily discernible to the quick eye. The gentle rise in slow water, or the swifter rush where the fly is in the current, starts a ripple immediately from the centre made by the nose or mouth of the fish, and, of course, is unmistakable where the actual taking of the insect is seen. In all cases the surface is broken. The commotion made by the bulging fish is started under water, and, while the disturbance is ultimately seen upon the surface, the form it assumes is more of a swirl or boil and is quite unlike the concentric rings that mark the actual breaking of the surface.

Occasionally, as I have said, the "fielder muffs the fly," and this is the moment that, if the angler be alert, an artificial fly dropped immediately over the fish is likely to meet with a hearty welcome. I am convinced that a trout that misses his prey in this manner frequently stays on

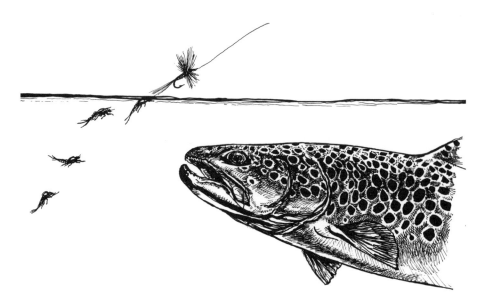

A quick cast, with the fly hitting the feeding fish right on the head, may take a fish that is bulging to emergers, but the angler "must be prompt in making the throw . . . because the fish may have his attention attracted elsewhere at any moment."

the spot where he lost it long enough to give the angler an opportunity to present his fly, if he is within striking distance—and ready. He must be prompt in making his throw, however, because the fish may have his attention attracted elsewhere at any moment. If a rise be not effected at once the angler should not try again immediately, because the possibility of the fish having left his position, or of having been scared by the line, or of frightening another which may have come between, is too great to make the attempt worth while.

When fish are feeding all over the pool, and the angler is impatient and not content to stand idly by waiting for an opportunity such as described, let him try the following method: He should look the water over carefully, keep out of it if possible, and choose the spot where the fly is to be placed. Knowledge of the water and of the habits of the fish will guide him in this choice, but he should not cast to the swirl. Having chosen his water, which should be toward the head of the pool, not much above its centre, and preferably where the current will carry the fly down faster than the leader (the choice being governed naturally by the character of the stretch), he should place his fly some distance—a yard or two— ahead of the swirl and a foot or two to the side nearest him, allowing it to float down eight or ten feet; if no rise is effected he should place his fly in the same spot again and agin until he has made twenty-five casts or more. It is important that each cast should be executed with the same precision and delicacy as marked the first attempt.

The method is based upon the theory that a feeding trout—or even one that is not feeding, for that matter— may be induced to take up a position in line with the direction in which the angler's fly is travelling, under the belief that flies are coming down-stream in such quantities as to make them worth investigating. Once this position is compelled it is only a question of time and patience upon the part of the angler. The trout will rise eventually to one of this "hatch." The angler cannot hope to have this *coup* come off, however, if he has made any mistake in his casting or has shown himself or his rod.

The beginner practising the method will find it most difficult to restrain an almost uncontrollable impulse to leave off casting in the one spot in order to place his fly over the swirl made by some other fish. If he gives way to that impulse he courts failure—and down comes the house he is building. It is quite likely that a trout is preparing to investigate the "hatch" at the very moment the angler changes his water, and, of course, will be frightened away by seeing the rod or the line which is thrown over it to the other fish. The method usually employed by the novice is productive of nothing. Because many feeding fish are seen, he hurriedly casts over this one, then over that one, in the hope that his fly will be taken, and finally gives up in despair when his hope is not realised.

If a mistake unfortunately occurs—the danger of which naturally increases in proportion to the number of casts made—it is quite useless to carry the attempt further. The angler should retire for a few moments or continue a bit farther up or down stream, selecting a spot some distance from where he began, and always bearing in mind the necessity for throwing above and to the near side of the swirl. If no mistake is made the chances are at least even that those early evening "rises" which have so long mocked his skill may show a profit. The angler, however, may spend a profitable quarter hour watching the insects upon the water or rising from it, and catching some for closer examination. During this time, if there is a cessation of swirls, as there likely will be, it indicates that the nymphae are becoming fewer and that, the "hatch" being over for the present, his last chance has come for a try at the bulgers. He should proceed, as before, to create his artificial "hatch," and he will have even a better chance of success because the attention of the trout will be less occupied.

In selecting water in which to place the fly, in order to take bulging fish by the method I have suggested, the angler will do well to choose that where the current is swift but the surface unbroken; and too much stress cannot be laid upon the importance of having the fly float down as nearly as possible in the same lane and position each time. When the trout have ceased feeding upon the nymphae his opportunity for casting to fish that are really rising is come, and he may try these until darkness drives him home.

One who has observed trout feeding upon the tiny *Diptera* called indiscriminately by anglers "black gnats," "punkies," "midges," etc., is quite inclined to believe that, while "smutting" is rather an inelegant term to apply to the fish, the insects themselves, considering the provocation, have been let off too lightly in being described as "smuts" and "curses." These diminutive pests seem to be abroad at all times of the day, but are particularly numerous in the late afternoon, when clouds of them may be seen hovering over the still water of the pools. At such times the trout seem to be busily feeding, but the keenest observation does not disclose what it is they are taking. These "curses" are so small that it seems incredible that large trout should be interested in them. That they are is easily proven by autopsy, and I have found solid masses of them in the gullets and stomachs of sizable fish, proving that they must have been extremely busy if the insects were taken singly. If one could see these tiny things upon the water, and could see a trout rise to them, he would have convincing evidence that they are taken singly; but, though my eyesight is still good, I have never been able to satisfy myself that I have actually seen a fish take one of them. After many experiences with trout under such conditions, and particularly after a series of observations extending on one occasion over a period of four successive days, I am almost ready to believe that the fish do not wait for them to fall upon the water. This notion—perhaps fanciful—came to me while on a pool that had been my objective during an afternoon's fishing, and upon which I intended to close the day. Arriving there about a half hour before sundown, I was not a little delighted to find fish rising freely all over. After studying them for a few moments I concluded that they were not "bulging," because the surface was broken each time with a distinct "smack." They could not have been "tailing," because the water was about four feet deep. They were not rising to any insects that I could see, although I looked long and steadily. Yet they rose freely, and each fish rose again and again in practically the same spot.

Using the smallest fly that I had with me, a flat-winged "black gnat" tied on a No. 16 hook, I cast faithfully but unavailingly for some time, endeavoring to interest two fish which were nearest me, and until I was quite ready to confess myself beaten. However, I decided to try them with a larger fly, and while preparing to tie this on my attention was attracted by four distinct clouds of insects hovering over the water—on the wing, certainly, but making no flight. They were merely dancing in the air about two feet above the pool. Watching closely, I saw the insects gradually decrease this distance until but an inch or two separated the lower extremity of a cloud of them from the water, when directly underneath would come another "smack" as the tail of a trout broke the surface. Immediately the swarm would scatter, though but for an instant, collecting again to perform the same evolution as before, when again they would be scattered by a fish under them. This happened to all four swarms in rapid succession, and it was quite evident that a trout was under each. Every time the insects were close to the water the tail of a trout would be seen and water would be thrown amongst them. Query: Did the trout deliberately throw water at these insects with the intention of drenching those within reach and in order that they might be picked up at leisure after they had fallen into the stream? And, if so, why were the fish not observed in the act of picking them up? Or did the sight of the insects excite the anger of the fish, or a sport-loving instinct—if, indeed, fish are capable of these emotions?

My subsequent experience with these fish tended

"Did the trout deliberately throw water at these insects with the intention of drenching those within reach?"

only to confuse me further in my guessing. This "spattering" game went on for fifteen or twenty minutes, and was brought to a conclusion, finally, by the retirement of the "curses," which left the scene perpendicularly, going straight up until lost to view. After they had disappeared the fish stopped rising. Having marked them down, I determined to have one more try with a large fly, and, to my amazement, my first cast brought a swift rise, but no connection was made. Resting the fish for a moment, I tried him again; he rose, and I was fast in what appeared to be a very good fish. I had great difficulty in leading him to the lower end of the pool, so that I might not disturb the others, and finally netted him. He proved to be a small trout and was hooked on the side just above the tail. I then tried the others, and, although I rose each one at least three times, I hooked none, nor on any occasion did I feel that the fly had been touched. By this time it was quite dark and I left for home.

On the three following days I met with the same experience. I had innumerable rises to my fly after the "curses" had left, hooked but one fish each evening, and, by a remarkable coincidence, each foul and near the tail. Again, query: Was this mere accident or were the trout trying to drench my fly? Were they still on the lookout for the sport afforded them by the clouds of insects? The gullets of the fish taken were lined with the small insects, the stomachs also being well filled with them; but how the fish took them after they had risen without my seeing some indication of it, I cannot imagine. I feel quite certain that they were not taken at the instant of the rise, because the insects did not touch the water at any time; nor did the trout show any part of their bodies above the surface except their tails. So they could not have been taken in the air. Some day, perhaps, the problem may be solved, but at present I have no solution to offer.

A bulging or smutting fish and a cursing angler are not a rare combination. If there is anything more perplexing and vexing than the sight of fish rising all about and one's best efforts going unrewarded, I cannot imagine what it is.

A bulging fish may be taken with an imitation of the insects he is feeding upon, either sunk in one form or floating in another; but a smutting fish cannot be appealed to with any imitation of his food of the moment. The colour of the pests may be imitated, but no ingenuity of man can fashion an artificial so that it will resmble in size the minute form of the natural; and, even if ingenuity could do it, the hook to be used in conformity would be absolutely useless and probably quite as difficult to make as the fly. Lacking a correct imitation of the "curses," which, even if good, might not be taken, one may accept the rebuffs offered to his fly with an equanimity born of the knowledge that he is not alone in his trouble.

If smutting fish are to be taken at all they will probably be taken on a fly that has no resemblance to any particular insect except, perhaps, one that is indigenous to the stream, or one in which the angler has faith. It may assume any form, flat-winged or erect. Colour, of course, is not important, except that it should not be too brilliant; a fly of sombre hue, such as the Whirling Dun, Cahill, or Evening Dun, being very effective, the Gold-Ribbed Hare's Ear or Wickham's Fancy frequently being accepted. I am inclined to think that a small fly receives no more attention than a large one, if as much; but nothing larger than a No. 12 or No. 14 hook should be used.

Meeting with failure while the insects are about, the angler should rest until they have disappeared and then, having marked the position of the fish, try them with the method described for bulgers. Failing again, let him figure it out if he can.

When fish are feeding upon some particular species of insect it is quite logical to assume that an imitation of that species will appeal to them more readily than an imitation of any other. But when the insects are numerous, as they are on occasions, and the fish are moving about, the chance of the artificial fly being selected from among the great number of naturals upon the water is one to whatever the number may be. As a general rule, the larger fish take up positions which by virtue of might are theirs for the choosing and almost invariably in places where many flies are carried down by the current. If they be rising steadily the angler is enabled to reduce the odds against him by his ability to place his fly near the spot where he knows one to be lying. It does not follow, however, that because certain insects are observed flying about they are of the species with which the trout are engaged for the moment.

If an insect be observed flying as though it had some objective point in view, it may be safely concluded that it has but recently assumed the winged state. In this case it is attractive to the fish only at the moment it emerges from its shuck, or immediately afterward while it is resting upon the water, for the very obvious reason that it does not appear upon the water again until it is about to deposit its eggs, if a female, or, if of the opposite sex, when it falls lifeless after the fulfilment of its natural duties.

When the insects are seen dancing about over the water, oftentimes a considerable height above it—in some cases thirty feet or more—the observer may be quite satisfied that they are the perfect males of the species waiting for the females to appear. After the sexual function has been completed the female may be seen flitting over the water, dipping to the surface and rising again, in the act of depositing her eggs, finally coming to rest as the function is completed, only to be swept away to her death. As she does not travel any considerable distance during this last act of her life, she proves of greatest interest to the fish at this stage of it.

One who observes closely will see that at the moment the female approaches the water, or during her subsequent dips, attempts, frequently successful, are made by the fish to capture her. As these efforts required some activity, they are resorted to usually by the more agile dandiprats. The larger fish are quite as interested in the dainty morsel as are their younger brothers, but they do not make the same frantic efforts to secure it, preferring to attend the fly closely in its movements until the opportunity presents itself to take it with little or no exertion. This is usually at the time ovipositing is about completed or the fly is resting upon the surface of the water preparatory to another flight. The females of some species are less active in the performance of this duty than those of others. They select the more placid stretches of the stream, ride quietly upon its surface, and the eggs exude from the oviduct as they sail along. Occasionally, after traveling in this manner for a time, they rise from the water, fly a short distance, and settle again. They are incapable of guiding themselves and are naturally carried along by the current and over the fish.

It has been my observation that during the period of ovipositing a great majority of the insects are headed directly up-stream, instinctively knowing, perhaps, that contact with the current in that position will more readily relieve them of their burdens. And, while I have no certain knowledge that it is so, I am inclined to believe that the setae or hair-like tail enables them to assume and maintain this position. At any rate, it should be the angler's ambition to imitate this action, and present his counterfeit with its tail or hook end coming down to the fish. This gives the added advantage of having the business end taken first and eliminates the danger of disturbing the fish by having the shadow of the leader thrown over him in advance. To do it successfully calls for a nice-

Egg-laying insects fly upstream and touch the water to dislodge their eggs. "It should be the angler's ambition to imitate this action, and present his counterfeit with its tail or hook end coming down to the fish."

ty of judgment in the handling of rod and line; but when the skill is acquired its successful execution has its own reward.

The utmost caution should be used in approaching a feeding fish. The danger of putting him down does not depend solely upon his getting sight of the angler; he may also be apprised of the angler's coming by the excited darting up-stream of smaller fish which have been below him. If the character of the water to be fished indicates that other and smaller fish may be hidden, or if their presence be disclosed by *their* feeding, it is much safer to cast at right angles to the selected fish than to attempt to cast from below and over the smaller ones. If the situation demands that the fly be placed from this position it should be floated to the fish from a point two or three feet above and should not be cast directly over him. Inasmuch as the trout is more likely to see the rod at this angle, a longer line should be thrown than would otherwise be necessary and, if the fish has been well spotted, great care must be exercised in presenting the fly without undue accompaniment of leader.

The fly may be presented alone by using the horizontal cast. If an attempt is being made to drop the fly three feet above the fish, it is necessary to aim at a spot six feet above, with a bit longer line than will just reach, suddenly checking the cast at the very end as it straightens. This will have the effect of throwing the fly down-stream. The leader will describe a sharp curve and follow after, and will not be seen by the fish before he sees the fly. After the fly has alighted, the rod should be held consistently pointed directly at the fly and in a horizontal position. Held in this way, it is less likely to be seen by the fish and a better control of the line is had if a rise be effected.

There are, in fact, good reasons why the rod should be held horizontally whenever and wherever the floating

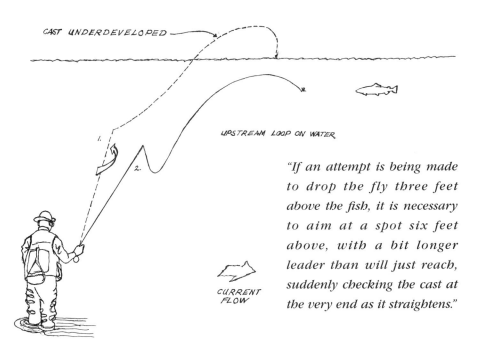

CAST UNDERDEVELOPED

UPSTREAM LOOP ON WATER

1.

2.

CURRENT FLOW

"If an attempt is being made to drop the fly three feet above the fish, it is necessary to aim at a spot six feet above, with a bit longer leader than will just reach, suddenly checking the cast at the very end as it straightens."

fly is being used, the line being stripped in by the unoccupied hand as much as may be necessary to keep the fly under control.

If the current be rapid between the angler and the fish, he should use a foot or two more of line and try to throw a larger curve in the leader so that the fly may reach the fish before drag is exerted upon it. If the cast be well done there is at least an even chance that the fly will be taken; if not well done, no move should be made to retrieve the fly until it has floated some distance below the fish, and even then the retrieve should not be made directly from the water with the full length of line. The line, leader, and fly will be swept down-stream at a speed depending upon the current, and will be approaching the angler's bank. By stripping the line in slowly and carefully, the fly may be lightly whisked off with little or no disturbance of the surface when there is

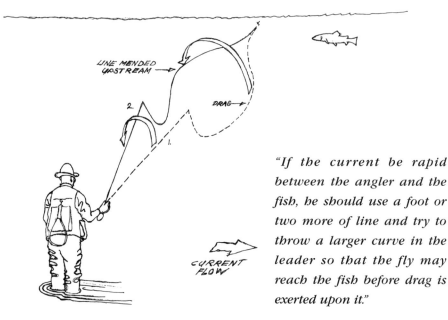

"*If the current be rapid between the angler and the fish, he should use a foot or two more of line and try to throw a larger curve in the leader so that the fly may reach the fish before drag is exerted upon it.*"

little but the leader upon the water, and another attempt made. The angler may continue this process as long as he feels he has made no mistake.

If the fly has been refused after a number of casts, and the fish continues to rise, it is some consolation to know that he has not been disturbed by the casting. A change of tactics is very often effective in such cases; and, if the fly be placed very close to the fish instead of being floated down to him, its sudden appearance, giving but little time for investigation, may cause him to rise to it.

When a rising fish may be cast to without disturbing those below him, the angler is in a more favourable position. Where practicable, the effort should be to make the throw with the leader curved and above the fly. Naturally, this is more easily accomplished when the fish—looking up-stream—is on the angler's left hand. Unless one be ambidextrous, or skilful enough to throw with the right hand from over the left shoulder, a fish under the right-hand bank is difficult to reach in this manner. Until the cast has been mastered, no attempt should be made to throw the curve; but one need not despair of taking fish in this position, even though this skill be lacking. The fly may be thrown straight, but from a more obtuse angle; and if, instead of being placed directly over or above the fish, it be placed slightly above and a foot to the near side of the spot where he rose, the danger of scaring him off with the leader is lessened, and the chance of his taking it not a bit.

Where a long cast is required, the line should never be extended to the length required to reach the fish. The distance should be measured carefully, and, when the fly in the false or air casts reaches a point five or six feet from the fish, that much line—which should be stripped from the reel and held in the left hand—should be allowed to pass through the guides on the next forward cast. This is called shooting the line. Not only is it of great assistance in attaining accuracy, but the momentum imparted to the "live" line, that part already clear of the top, is lost and does not travel down to the fly, which, shorn of impulse, remains suspended for an instant above the water and falls thereon as lightly as the proverbial feather.

The fly should never be aimed directly at the water, but at an imaginary point three or four feet above, and a like distance in advance of, the spot it is desired to reach. This direction must be implicitly observed in this method of casting, because the fly will invariably fall short unless a greater length of line be used than is apparently necessary. Very often the fly will fall heavily if just the required length of line is used without "shooting."

Where a fish is rising in the strong current, a short line, not over twenty-five feet, will be sufficient and quite enough to handle, as it is returned very quickly to the angler. In this case the "shoot" may be abandoned in the actual delivery of the fly and used only to lengthen the line between casts after the retrieve, which should be made only when the fly has passed considerably behind the fish—the exact distance naturally being determined by the circumstances. The line should be stripped with the left hand to keep pace with the speed with which the fly travels and no faster, else its action will not be natural. Nothing but the fly and leader should be on the water, and as little of the latter as possible. Get behind the fish, but do not cast directly over him. The fly should come down past him to one side or the other, with the leader always on the same side—away from the fish.

Early in the season, if the weather be propitious and the stream in good condition, it is not unlikely that fish will be seen rising throughout the day—perhaps not all of the time but often enough to keep the angler alert. The fact that they are rising at all is quite sufficient to arouse his interest, because, even though the fish nearest him does not take his fly, the one above may; and, all things considered, he may hope to have a fairly interesting day, with the further chance, if fortune smiles, of a good one.

How different the situation confronting the angler who elects to fish the streams in the hot summer months, with the water at its lowest mark, clear as crystal—or gin, as the Englishman has it—and not a fish to be seen rising the whole livelong day, for the very good reason that no insects are about to offer inducement. Even in June these conditions sometimes prevail, with the redeeming feature, however, that toward evening the falling temperature, or the approach of darkness, or both, seem to induce a rise of insects, with an accompanying rise of trout. The angler, having patiently waited for this time, sets hard at work and is content to take a couple of fair fish in the hour or so before dark.

I confess to a certain weakness for the stream during those periods of extreme heat when the local experts agree that it is almost impossible to take fish. Actuated, perhaps, as much by a desire to take a good fish as by the hope of learning whether or not their theories were correct, I have gone to the stream under such conditions and have had some curious experiences. I have taken fine fish on broiling hot days when there seemed to be little difference between the temperature of the water and the air. On days when the "hatch" has been so thin that one would be warranted in thinking that the trout had forgotten that there ever was such a thing as a fly, I have taken some of my best fish. On the other hand, there have been many occasions when I have met with utter defeat, and, all in all, I hardly know what I have really learned from the experiences, so varied have they been.

One insufferably hot July day convinced me, however, that there are times when trout are interested neither in food nor in anything else. For three sultry hours I cast over every likely spot. I never rose a fish. I never saw one rise. I did not see a fish.

At a beautiful pool, small but of good depth, considering the state of the water, I felt that my last chance had come, and after covering the whole surface carefully, without result, deliberately waded into it, hoping to scare any fish that might be there and so learn where they were hiding. I did not see a fin, and had about decided it was tenantless, when, looking down, I saw, close to my feet, the tail of a fish sticking out from under a small boulder. I looked under the up-stream side of the boulder, hoping to see the fish's head, but could not, as there was no hollow on that side. I gently stroked that part of the fish in sight with the tip of my rod, and received in acknowledgment a gentle waving of the tail. Placing my gear behind me in the dry bed of the stream, I proceeded to move the boulder to see what manner of trout this might be. Not until I had it completely removed did he stir—and then he moved but a short distance to a similar hiding-place. He was a brown trout about fifteen inches long, and so sluggish was he that it would have been the simplest matter to have seized him with my hands.

A short distance above the pool there is a dam famous for the big trout which make their home under it. I covered the water faithfully, without success, and, after I had finished, crawled out upon the apron of the dam. Peering into the pool below, I saw, directly underneath me, eighteen or twenty trout ranging from six inches in length to one old "lunker" over twenty. As this spot had been cast over repeatedly, and apparently without any glaring error, I felt in no humour to try again, but determined to test their appetites in another way. Catching a half dozen grasshoppers, I dropped one in front of the big fish that led the school. He paid not the slightest attention to it. Neither did any of the others, not even the smallest one. I tried again, throwing another grasshopper a bit upstream so that it would float down in plain view for a longer time, and again provoked no interest upon the part of the fish. Finally, I killed one of the grasshoppers, crushing it so that it would sink, and threw it well above the fish. It came down under water directly on a line with the big fish, which deliberately moved a bit to one side, apparently to avoid having it touch him. Each fish behind him did the same thing, even the smallest ones ignoring it.

Now, what sort of a fly, wet, sunk, or dry, or, if the angler was inclined to try it, what sort of bait could he use to interest such fish? Under the conditions then prevailing—the thermometer recording 94 degrees in the shade, the stream at its lowest point, and the temperature of the water very high—I really believe that the only chance he might have had would have been with a very "wet" mint julep. Under the circumstances it would have required considerable self-denial to have offered that. This heat was exceptional, however, and fishing in such weather is quite as trying as fishing in the cold, blustering days of early spring. In either case, even if fish are taken, enthusiasm is not greatly aroused on the part of either angler or trout.

I confess I do not know what method of fly fishing one may use to entice a trout when the temperature is extreme, because when the fish is found under a boulder, as he probably will be, he will not see a floating fly, and it is almost hopeless to expect a sunken fly to attract any attention—witness the case of the idle fish and the grasshoppers. If fish not hiding in caverns refuse live grasshoppers dropped directly in front of their noses, it is quite evident that there is small chance of taking them on any sort of artifical lure.

Leaving out of consideration, however, the few periods of unbearable heat, that part of the season between June 15 and August 31 may have many days rich in experience for the angler, and even though there be many days when the fish will be found not to be rising to natural insects, the pleasure derivable from trying for success is commensurate with the difficulty of approaching and luring them.

When the streams are low and clear great circumspection and care are required in approaching fish or likely places and in presenting the fly. The slightest error will be detected at once, and subsequent attempts to interest the fish will be effort merely wasted.

The angler who carefully casts over and thoroughly fishes a likely piece of water should not come too quickly to the conclusion that it contains no fish. If it happens to be one of those days (too frequent in the experience of the present-day angler) when a great length of stream may be traversed without his seeing the slightest indication of a rising fish, he may, of course, if he be so inclined, comfort himself with the thought that the fish are not feeding and abandon his fishing. But I hope to show that upon just such days the proper use of the dry fly will measure the difference between an empty creel and some success, even though that success be limited to the probability of a single good fish.

An English dry fly angler fishing our Eastern American streams by rote and casting only over or to rising fish would have many empty days to record in his diary. Days and days might pass without his seeing the "dimple" of a big fish or even the splash of a small one, except, possibly, just at dusk; and at such times his skill and patience would be taxed as heavily as ever by any smutting fish of a chalk stream. But does it follow, as some authorities seem to have suggested, that because a fish is not risen by a few casts here and there it has no inclination to come to the surface or that such inclination may not be aroused? I think not, my experience having proven the contrary.

The entire theory of forcing the fish to rise to the fly is based upon the fact that a trout may be decoyed from the position occupied by it when not feeding to one fixed by the angler, provided, of course, the fish is not asked to come any great distance. The practice of the method necessitates considerable knowledge of the fish and of the character of the places it frequents. The fly cast, say, twenty times, in close proximity to the supposed lair of a fish, in nine cases out of ten will prove more effective than twice the same number of casts placed indiscriminately over the water. But no glaring mistake, such as undue splashing or frantic waving of the rod, is overlooked by the fish. If such errors have been

"The single fly should be placed a foot or two from the spot where the fish is supposed to be and to one side of it" to create a hatch by casting near a trout twenty or thirty times.

committed, the angler had best retire and try some fish that has not become acquainted with him.

Having chosen the point of vantage from which to assail the fish, which choice should be governed, first, by reason of its being out of range of the trout's vision, and then by the availability of casting room behind—note the order of importance—the single fly should be placed a foot or two from the spot where the fish is supposed to be and to one side of it. The instructions given in regard to casting to bulging fish so as to produce the effect of a hatch should be followed to the letter. Even where the distance seems rather too far to expect the fish to travel, it is better to select water that flows continuously in one direction in which to place the fly. It is preferable to have the fly travel in one "lane" during its promemade, rather than to have its action marred by a possible drag resulting from an attempt to get it closer to the fish. If the fly has been natural in its action, it is quite likely that it has attracted the attention of the fish, and the angler may at any moment be amazed to see a trout backing slowly down-stream under it, seemingly coming from nowhere. This is the trying time, as the fish, having come closer to the angler, is more likely to be frightened off by any sudden movement; but if the angler is careful, the satisfaction of eventually seeing the fish rise deliberately and fasten to the fly is not to be measured by that of taking a larger fish by any other method.

Great care should be exercised in retrieving the fly from the water, because a fish taking up a position under the angler's lane of flies usually backs down-stream a bit. In no case should the fly be retrieved until it has floated down to a point nearly at right angles to or even below the rod. Strict observance of this rule will prevent scaring off many fish that might otherwise be induced to rise.

Where the swiftness of the current precludes any possibility of preventing drag, particularly in those miniature pools behind rocks in the centre of the stream called "pockets," the fly may be placed lightly thereon, and as lightly whished away, being left but an instant, to be returned immediately and often, until the angler is satisfied that the pocket contains no fish, or that he is unable to interest them if it does. In any event, he need not feel that an opportunity has been lost to him because of his inability to avoid drag, for in this sort of water the error is not always observed by the fish.

There can be no question but that stalking a feeding fish and finally taking him on an artificial fly affords sport of the highest quality. The taking of a fish that may be seen but is not feeding, either because of lack of food or disinclination, is quite as difficult to accomplish, however, and is productive of equally good sport.

I relate the following story of the taking of a trout

under almost impossible conditions, not so much to illustrate the success of the method as to show the satisfaction that attends the accomplishment of the feat. This individual fish is only one of many that I have taken similarly in the many years that I have fished with the floating fly, and the history of its taking is given here because it illustrates and bolsters up my claim that the dry fly repeatedly cast over a sluggish, non-feeding fish will induce him to rise.

The last two days of the season of 1909, August 29 and 30, found me on the banks of the Kaaterskill, at Palenville, Greene County, N.Y. This stream is a brawling one, resembling many Rocky Mountain streams, and some magnificent rainbow trout inhabit it; yet in six hours' fishing, one afternoon, I raised but one good-sized fish, in which I left my fly. The dozen or more fish from ten to twenty inches in length which could be seen restlessly swimming about in each of the pools appeared to be interested in nothing but a desire to escape the intense heat, and at length I abandoned the sport as hopeless.

A gentlemen who had once lived in that section, and who had fished the streams of the surrounding country for over thirty years, invited me to fish a stream some miles away with him the next day. I accepted his invitation, and the morning found us on the banks of what should have been the Plattekill, but proved to be nothing but a mere trickle. With many misgivings I started in, my companion going up-stream about a mile to fish down and meet me.

The only likely water within three or four hundred yards was a pool under a dam, and here I rose and pricked a good fish. Leaving him, I cut across a neck of land to meet my companion at the turn, and found him ready to quit. But I determined to try again for the fish I had risen, and, while following the stream back, discov-

ered a pool against the bank, some eight feet wide and
not over a dozen in length, with six feet of water in it. On
the bottom lay a fine brown trout, as motionless as if
dead. He was actually lying on the sand and pebbles,
apparently devoid of all interest in life. I withdrew quietly
and, getting below him and behind a tree-stump on the
bank, put on a new fly—a Whirling Dun—and, with but
little hope, sent the fly on its errand. It fell lightly upon
the glassy surface about a yard above the fish, which was
at all times in plain view; but he seemed entirely oblivi-
ous to it. There was practically no current to carry it
down, and it seemed an interminable length of time
before the fly got below the fish far enough for me to
take it off the water without disturbance; but at last I
retrieved it and, after drying it thoroughly, dropped it
again. I repeated this operation six times before I noticed
any change in the position of the fish, and all of the time
he was just "lolling" on the bottom. The sixth cast seemed
to attract his attention, and, with all fins moving, he lifted
ever so little from the bottom and stood poised. I felt that
I had him interested—that he was alert—and I knew that
the slightest mistake from then on meant failure, compete and certain; and my excitement was not helping a
bit. Another cast, and I imagined I could see him tremble;
at any rate, his fins moved rapidly, but without imparting
any motion to the body, except to lift it an inch or two
toward the surface. Each succeeding cast brought the
same excited action of the fins and tempted him a few
inches nearer the surface. I thought he never would
reach the top, and felt that if he didn't get within his distance soon I would bungle the whole affair. At last, and
after I had made more than twenty-five casts, he had
risen to within six inches of the surface; as the fly was
presented again, he made a determined rush, stopping
just short of it and allowing it to float over him, apparent-

ly without further interest. I gently retrieved the fly, though I felt that it was all over, as the fish had probably detected the fraud. However, I made another cast and the fly fortunately alighted softly. The fish made the same rush, refusing it as before; but after the fly had floated down a foot or so, he turned slowly and deliberately down-stream, and, rising quietly, took the fly with a distinct "suck," turned to go down with it, and was fast.

This was not a very large trout—fifteen inches or so—but his taking afforded more genuine sport than a dozen larger ones might have yielded taken in any other way, because of the circumstances under which it was accomplished. I may have had a possible advantage over him, because a floating fly had, probably, never been cast on the stream before. Aside from this fact, it cannot be said that the element of luck entered into the affair at all, except, perhaps, in so far as it enabled me to deliver my fly so many times without mistake. I have, however, taken many other and larger fish in practically the same manner and by the employment of the same tactics, and know the method to be sound in theory and practice. For the solace of the beginner who may attempt to practise the method, let me add that in the beginning the fish I took were, probably, a very small number of those from which all thoughts of feeding were driven by my bungling.

If a trout lying in a small pool and in plain view, as was the one whose story has just been told, could be induced to come up through six feet of water to take the fly, is it not fair to assume that an unseen fish may also be forced to rise by the same tactics? Of course, in the case of an unseen fish, the angler labours under some disadvantage, because he is casting somewhat in the dark. In addition to ability to deliver many casts perfectly to a selected spot, he must also have the experience and knowledge that enable him to decide, at least approximately, where the fish may lie under the prevailing conditions. If his judgment in this particular is at fault his chances of rising the fish are gone. He should, therefore, assume that it occupies any of three or four positions, and for his first cast should choose that one of them which may be cast over with the least danger of disturbing the fish should it occupy any one of the others. If a rise be not had after a certain number of casts over the chosen position, the others should each be fished in turn.

The chance of putting down a fish for good will increase in proportion to the number of casts over each position, multiplied by the number of positions. That a rise is not had from the position first chosen will not prove that a fish does not occupy it, and the angler's subsequent casts will be made under increased difficulty, because of his efforts to refrain from further disturbing that water.

Before leaving this subject, and at the risk of becoming somewhat tedious and tiring my reader, I will relate the circumstances of the taking of an unseen fish by repeatedly casting over a chosen spot—in other words, of "forcing a rise." The incident has an added interest because a fellow angler witnessed it and was thereby convinced that a fish could be moved into position by the fly.

We were fishing the Brodhead, in Pennsylvania. It was in July and the day was very hot. The water was extremely low and very clear, and the upper reach of the stream just below the Canadensis bridge, which we had elected to fish, did not look big enough to hold a trout of any size. In one particular stretch there was a hundred yards of very shallow water, a small pocket on the right-hand bank being the only likely looking spot. I knew this stretch held many fine fish when the stream was in better condition, and I decided that this particular pocket might be the abiding-place of a good trout. As it was

approaching the noon hour, I determined to go no farther up-stream but to spend a half hour experimenting
on the little pocket.

The surface of the miniature pool was not over eight
feet wide anywhere no more than that in length, but its
depth below a jutting rock which formed one side of it
convinced me that it was worth trying, although there
was no actual indication that a fish occupied it. The bottom was plainly discernible except in the swifter water
near the head, and, as no fish could be seen, I selected
the edge of this swift water upon which to place my fly.
A dozen or more casts were made without any apparent
effect, when suddenly a yellow gleam at the tail of the
pocket, just after the fly had floated over the lip, disclosed a fine trout poised in the flattening water.
Explaining the situation to my companion—who was
now all excitement, having seen the fish, and who really
did not believe it could be taken—on the spur of the
moment I decided to try to prove my theory at the risk
of losing the fish. I ceased casting to him. We watched
him for probably two or three minutes, during which
time he appeared to be keenly alert, when he quietly left
his position and moved back up-stream into the swift
water and out of sight. My opportunity had come,
although my friend thought I had lost it. To make more
certain that the colour of the fly played no part in the
affair, I substituted a Silver Sedge for the Whirling Dun I
had been using. After about a dozen casts with this fly
there came the same yellow gleam, and the fish was back
into position again. This time I continued casting, and,
although he seemed to "lean" toward the fly each time it
came down, he did not take it until it had passed by ten
times, finally rising deliberately and fastening on the
eleventh cast. He proved to weigh one pound ten
ounces.

To what conclusion does the observation of this fish bring us? If he had been ready to feed before the artificial appeared, is it likely that he would have permitted it to pass over or near him a score of times before taking? And when he occupied what I call his feeding position, why did he allow the fly to pass ten times, although exhibiting a certain interest in it each time? It was never beyond his reach and could easily have been taken. Was the desire to feed being gradually aroused in him at each sight of the fly? When he did take it, it was done with such certainty that he must have believed it to be a natural, although quite unlike anything he had recently seen. One thing is certain, however. He was decoyed from one position to another on two occasions within a few minutes of each other, and by a different pattern of fly each time.

CHAPTER IV
WHERE AND WHEN TO FISH

The swift streams in the eastern part of the United States must, as a rule, be fished by wading. Where it is possible, because of the absence of trees and brush, to fish from the bank, the angler's form is silhouetted sharply against the background of sky, and, to overcome this disadvantage, he must retire some distance from the edge of the bank, or, if he wishes to come closer, must kneel or crouch to avoid being seen by the fish. By casting from the bank he will avoid the disturbance of the water necessarily made by entering it, and this is, of course, an advantage. On the other hand, he is closer to the surface of the stream while wading, in which position he is not so easily seen, which is also an advantage. Offsetting the latter, however, is the commotion made by his movements, which, no matter how deliberate, will make the trout nervous or apprehensive of approaching danger. If he has shown himself, even though the fish has been vigorously feeding, he might just as well abandon any attempt to induce a rise, because the trout, having been warned by his careless approach, will have scurried away. The danger of putting down a fish in swift water is not so great because the ripples sent in advance of the angler make little headway and travel no great distance against a strong current.

To describe places where trout may be looked for under any and all circumstances, is practically impossible. Very often the fish will not be found where the angler thinks they should be. They are as full of notions and idiosyncrasies as anglers themselves, and one may hope to become familiar with their habitat in a general way only, and this after close study. I say "in a general way," because, while a big trout may be known to inhabit a certain pool, it does not follow that he is in the same spot to-day that he occupied yesterday or the day before. He may be looked for somewhere about, but a distance of even three or four feet from his previous known position may so place him as to prevent the angler from approaching without being seen. I am speaking of fish that are not rising. Of course, if they should be feeding upon the surface they are easily spotted.

Each pool or piece of water should be examined carefully after it has been fished. In this way the deeper holes, the nooks under the banks, and the crevices between boulders are discovered and marked down. If the angler is to spend much time on a stream that is new to him, it is even permissible to enter the deeper water quietly for the purpose of a thorough investigation; but under no circumstances should this be done if other anglers are upon the stream. As a rule, we are too careless of others' rights, and the ethics of fly fishing should be observed quite as closely as the code that governs our actions in any other sport.

A long, flat stretch of the stream is likely to contain many big fish, and must be approached in the most circumspect manner. The angler who hopes to take one of them should study the water carefully before entering it, and strive to determine just where the biggest fish lie. The character of the water and its temperature and the prevailing weather conditions are the data from which he must make his deductions.

By way of illustration, let us assume that the angler is

upon the stream, prepared to fish it.

The day is one somewhere between the first of May and the fifteenth of June. It is not too bright, and a light wind with a touch of summer in it is blowing up-stream. The water is running down after a light rain, and while not crystal clear is not much discoloured. It is about five-thirty o'clock of the afternoon, and the trout from below the stretch are coming on the feed. The flat to be fished is about one hundred and fifty feet long from where the water flows into it to where it rolls out again at the tail, and about fifty feet wide where the banks are farthest apart, narrowing, fan-like, to ten feet or less at the head. The current, gliding silently along the left bank (looking up-stream), shows the deep water to be on that side. These are ideal conditions, of course, and I have chosen them for that very reason. The angler is indeed fortunate who happens upon the stream when they prevail.

The natural place to look for trout under such conditions is anywhere along the left bank in the deep water. If flies are hatching—as in all probability they will be at this season—the angler need but watch for the rise that will indicate the position of the feeding fish. If these fish be small, as will be evidenced by the "staccato smack" made as the fly is taken, he should move farther up-stream, because no really big feeding fish need be looked for where small ones are: *vice versa*, little fish rarely feed in the same place and at the same time as big ones. If no rise is seen, the task then is to locate the fish, and, under the favourable conditions prevailing, it may be fairly assumed that they are ready to feed. There will be one place in the flat where more surface food collects than in any other, and one place where more comes down-stream because of converging current. In one of such places the biggest fish will be found.

Wherever an eddy swirls gently against a small cove

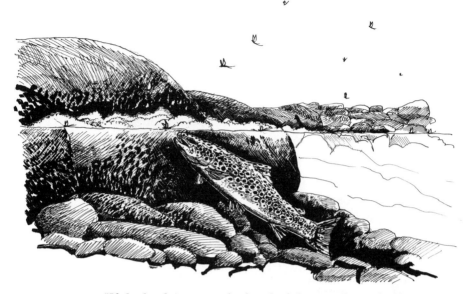

"If the backwater at the head of the stretch is of an area great enough to collect and hold the foam made by the tumbling water, this is the spot from which the angler may hope to secure one of the best fish in the pool, if not the best."

in the bank, or the force of the current spends itself against a rock, making a dead water or backwater above it, the fly may search and find many fine trout. If the backwater at the head of the stretch is of an area great enough to collect and hold the foam made by the tumbling water, this is the spot from which the angler may hope to secure one of the best fish in the pool, if not *the* best. One of the favourite feeding positions of a large trout is under this foam, and the fly, placed carefully again and again, often tempts him to move into his feeding position when, at the beginning of the casting, he lay outside of it. The fly should be dropped lightly on the foam and permitted to remain there until it is snatched away by the current.

It may happen that this particular part of the stretch does not contain one very large fish that "lords it" over a considerable area, but a number of fair-sized ones which, if feeding, will be somewhat scattered, and should be looked for in each of the places described.

Before or after the foam, backwater, and eddies have been tried, preferably before, the water on either side of the swiftest part of the current should be cast over, the fly being placed just at the bottom and at the side of the

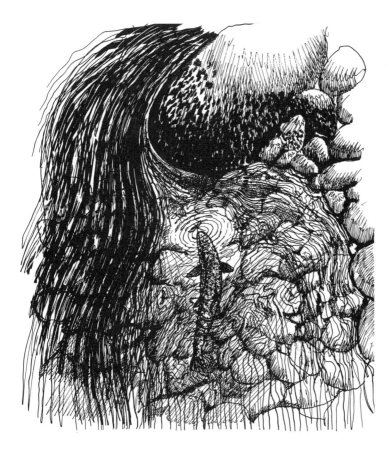

"The water on either side of the swiftest part of the current should be cast over, the fly being placed just at the bottom and at the side of the 'lumpy' water."

"lumpy" water. A fly cast to this position is extremely effective, dancing most naturally as it comes swiftly down-stream. This water should be tested thoroughly, the fly being placed always in the same spot and permitted to follow the same course for as long a distance as possible.

As daylight wanes, the fish often drop back to the tail of the stretch, sometimes feeding upon the very lip, or just above where the water begins to quicken before it spills out. This habit of trout may be due to their becoming less wary as dark approaches, and, consequently, quite willing to enter shallower water, where they find it easier to pick up a few insects or a minnow or two than in the deeper, swifter water above. Wherefore, if the angler has been unsuccessful at the head of the stretch, let him, by traveling circuitously, find a position some distance below the lip, and fish the still water carefully as

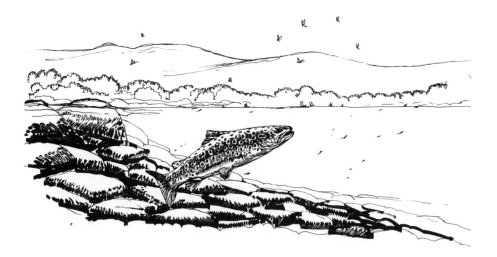

"As daylight wanes, the fish often drop back to the tail of the stretch, sometimes feeding at the very lip, or just above where the water begins to quicken before it spills out."

long as he can see his fly.

If the day is hot and bright, the water low and clear, and the fish not in any of the positions already described, they may be in either one of two places—along the bank or in the white water at the head.

If the fish are lying alongside of the bank they will prove to be as difficult to take as the most fastidious could wish. Knowledge of the crannies, depth, etc., will help the angler and make his task easier. But if the water is strange to him, and the trout must be searched for, his task is more complicated and he must exercise the greatest care in approaching. In many cases the stretches are

"If the day is hot and bright, the water low and clear, ... [trout] may be in either one of two places—along the bank or in the white water at the head."

lined on both sides by alders, willows, and the like, that make it impossible to cast without entering the water and, by so doing, forming ripples which, advancing ahead of the fly, warn the trout that danger is afoot. Exercising patience, he may walk slowly and quietly into the water at the tail of the stretch and as closely as possible to the bank the fish are under. Having attained the desired position, he should remain there long enough to allow all commotion made by his entry to cease, during which time no motion of the rod should be made, because the sight of any moving object will send the now alert trout scurrying, while the ripples will make him uneasy for a short time only. The horizontal cast should be used if possible. The fly should be floated down about a foot from the bank, and it should not be retrieved until it has travelled more than half the distance between the angler and the spot where it alighted. Casting should be continued until a mistake has marred the attempt, when the angler should desist, to resume after a short time has elapsed if the error has not been a glaring one.

When satisfied that no trout are within the section covered by the fly, the angler should lengthen his line and fish the fly a few feet above—always permitting the fly to travel over the water already fished. He should continue this until the maximum line that can be handled neatly without moving from the original position is being cast. When the line becomes unwieldy (in this method and position it is courting failure to attempt anything over thirty-five to forty feet, even if one is expert) an advance may be made a few yards up-stream as closely to the bank as the depth of the water and free casting space will permit. As it is quite possible—and likely, too—that a trout has been under the fly all the while, but was not interested in it, the angler's advance will drive him ahead, and indications of this should be sharply looked for. The discovery of the fish will save much valuable time, for in that case the immediate stretch may be abandoned, because any fish above the one seen will have certainly taken alarm at the actions of his fellow and will have lost all desire to feed for some time.

If no fish is disturbed, search the bank carefully along its length, always remembering to have the fly float down a considerable distance before retrieving. The chances are quite even, if the approach has been made carefully and quietly, that a good fish will be risen. In such water only skill of the highest type is rewarded. If it is not possible to follow along the bank under which the trout are lying, the cast may be made from the opposite side; but in this case a longer line should be used. If the water must be entered to reach the bank from the opposite side—and this, unfortunately, is usually the case—the angler should not move or allow his rod to move for some time after he has taken his position.

Having reached the head of the stretch, the angler may go over the eddies, backwater, and swift, and, if he meets with no response, the white water. This, above all places, is the difficult water to fish with the dry fly, and many anglers believe it to be quite impossible. If the dry fly be fished as is the wet fly—that is, cast in the swirl and allowed to drift about and down—it will become thoroughly drenched. But if it is placed properly and with due calculation, it is as easily kept dry and floating as upon any other part of the stream. The explanation lies in the fact that the fly is not placed directly upon the white water at all, if it be properly placed, but is cast to either side of the swift water, always on the side nearest the angler first, who should pick out the smooth looking spots upon which to place the fly. The fish which the wet fly angler takes directly from the centre of the current are taken on the dry fly by being induced to move out of

"This, above all places, is the difficult water to fish with the dry fly, and many anglers believe it to be quite impossible."

their position. A very short line is used, and the fly is floated but a foot or two, being dropped lightly again and again. I will admit that trout are not taken from the white water in this way by the dry fly as frequently as they are with the sunk fly, but when one *is* taken it is usually a good fish.

On either side of the brink of the miniature fall above the white water may be seen boulders, seemingly acting as gatemen, directing the running waters to pass between. The current gliding swiftly toward them, deflected to right and left, reminds one of a flock of sheep all trying to get through a gap in the fence at the same time, those caught against the edge of the opening making little headway; and so it is with that part of the current which spends most of its force against the boulders. If this water be examined it will be discovered that considerable dead or back water is formed under the surface just above the boulders. Such places are among the selected retreats of *Salmo fario*.

A fly floated down from a point two feet above and retrieved just as it is about to go over the fall may produce a very pretty picture for the angler. If the fly upon its first appearance has been seen by the trout, he is often induced to rush at it, and, missing, goes headlong over the fall, instinct telling him, perhaps, that he may find it below. Not to disappoint him, the angler drops it immediately at the edge of the white water, where it usually meets with a vicious reception. Should all not come off as planned, the fly may be cast again above the boulder and retrieved as before. The fish may be tempted to dart out and seize it after a dozen or more casts. If hooked, he will come over the fall to be dealt with in the smoother water below, and the angler will not have missed the picture, after all.

Native trout rarely occupy such positions, but they should never be overlooked in streams known to contain brown or rainbow trout.

Sometimes a short stretch of smooth, swift water will be found sweeping silently along the mossy bank just above the sentinel boulders at the head of the white water. The bank is probably shaded by overhanging rhododendron, or alder growth, that lends to the water a peculiar greenish hue. This stretch may be occupied by fine fish that, because of some effect of light or shade, seem better able to detect the approach of an angler or the connection of the leader with the fly than do fish in similar waters unshaded. A longer line is necessary here, and great care should be exercised to refrain, as far as possible, from entering that arc of a circle which is presumed to limit the range of the trout's vision. Difficulty will also be experienced in handling the line, owing to the greater length used and the rapidity with which it will be returned by the current. The danger of scaring the fish is minimised if the fly be delivered from a point almost directly in line with the current and the horizontal cast used. While not always necessary, the horizontal cast is better at all times, as the fly seems to cock more readily when thrown from this angle.

As a stretch of this character is usually of uniform depth along the greater part of its length, the fish may be in any part of it on a "feeding" day—a day when those below seemed to have been willing to feed. The fly should be placed at the foot of the stretch and on the side nearest the rod, and gradually worked, in the subsequent casts, toward the centre and head. This must be done slowly, however, and the fly should not be retrieved until it has come down some distance and has passed the spot where the first cast was delivered. The fish, in all probability, will be found near the middle of the stretch and to the side of the centre of the current nearer the bank. No attempt should be made to get closer, because the chance of having the fish come to the fly is greater than that of his taking after the line has been seen.

When the prevailing conditions indicate that the trout are not in the open—in other words, are not fully engaged in feeding or in looking for food—they will usually be found lying near the bank. In such cases, the first attempt should be made at the tail or down-stream end of the swift, the fly being gradually worked up-stream a foot or so at a time and about a foot from the bank. It should be allowed to drift down to the foot of the stretch each time, and the casting continued until the entire length of the bank has been thoroughly searched. If the bank should be of gravelly or earthy formation it may be an overhanging one, having been undermined by the action of the current. The angler may be certain that this is so if that part above water shows a mass or network of bared roots. In this case the same procedure is followed, with the exception that the fly should be placed two feet, or even more, from the edge of the tangle, so that it may come the better within the angle of the fish's vision. It is quite obvious that a fly placed too close to the bank will be unseen by a fish occupying the hollow under it. Great perseverance, even persistence, is required to induce a fish to leave a retreat of this sort in which he is snugly ensconced, but the attempt should not be abandoned while it is certain that no blunder has been made. Large trout love these places, and coaxing one out is worth a great deal of effort.

Long before a rise is effected, warning of the possibility of its coming off is given by the flash of a trout as he leaves his position under the bank to assume another under the lane or *hatch* of frauds. The trout is often a better judge of distance than the angler, and when this action of the fish is observed, any attempt to make it easier for him by placing the fly closer to the bank will, in all probability, put a stop to further interest on his part. Difficult as it is to disobey the impulse to place the fly where the fish was seen, it must be resisted, because, while there is a possibility that the fish may be risen, there is a greater likelihood that he will be put down. For this reason the original plan should be followed without deviation. Ask him to come to the fly, and, while he may seem diffident at first, he will finally accept the invitation.

These swifts, or runs, as they are termed, vary in length from fifteen to fifty feet, or more, and the greater their length the more difficult they are for the angler to cover without showing himself. They are the narrows of the stream, and, where the water is found to be of unvarying depth, the fish may be looked for in any part of them. The steady, rapid flow of the current is admirably adapted to the use of the floating fly, and is particularly attractive to those impatient ones who are unwilling to wait and watch the fly's slow progress on the quieter waters. Where the run being fished is distinctly "lumpy"—that is, where its speed is greater because of the sharper incline in the stream bed, and miniature waves are formed that hurry down one after another— the floating fly will be more difficult to handle, but is very effective if well placed.

It was once my good fortune to see a stretch of this character on the Neversink fished by a friend, Mr. Walter McGuckin, who has been my companion on many fishing excursions. He is one of the best hands with a rod that I have ever seen. His precision with the fly is remarkable, and I doubt if the grace and ease with which he handles his line can be excelled. His skill is fortified with a knowledge of trout gained by over thirty-five years' experience on the waters of New York State. And, by the by, although he has used the wet fly for the greater portion of this time, he will now take his fish on the dry fly or not at all.

The weather of four seasons has been crowded into a single day—and this at the end of May. Although no insects of any kind had been seen, we had been able to mark a fish down the day before, when he had shown himself for an instant. Having fished the smooth water on either side of the centre of the current without engaging the fish's attention, my friend decided to "ride his fly" on top of the waves in the very swiftest part of the current. To do this effectively, and without having too much of the leader on the water, the chance of exposing himself to the fish was taken, as the fly had to be delivered from almost a right angle. However, it all came off correctly, and the fly, seeming barely to touch the water as it danced along, appeared even more lifelike than a natural insect. So, too, it must have appeared to the trout, for, after a number of casts had been made, a fish leaped directly from one wave to the one above, upon which was the fly, took it with mouth wide open and dived under. He was led gently to the still water below, and, although he proved to be a fine brown trout, his manner of taking the fly appealed to us more than his quality, and he was returned to the stream. The rise is the thing, and a dashing one of this sort makes the blood quicken as the dull *chug* of a fish taking under water never can.

When a trout is taken on a floating fly from beneath the tangled rubbish which collects about the submerged roots of a fallen tree or stump, the angler may attribute his success to common sense and reason more than to his dexterity in placing the fly. If we assume that the fish is under the tangle, taking advantage of the shade and protection it affords, is it logical to expect him to worm his way up through it to take a fly? And, as his head is invariably pointed up-stream, is it at all likely that a fly placed behind him will be observed? The answer is obviously, no! When a trout occupies a position of this character, it is always because of its proximity to water which will permit him the greatest freedom in securing food or in escaping from danger. He is often unwilling, and frequently unable, to dart rapidly down-stream when moved by either of these considerations, and the fly should be so presented that it will ask nothing uncommon of him.

Many anglers fail to take fish from these justly famed and wisely chosen domiciles of big trout, because of their reluctance or inability to estimate the odds on or against the sporting proposition. They are not ready to risk a ten cent fly for the purpose of properly fishing a spot which has cost them a hundred times as much to reach. With a few desultory casts—placed, usually, where they will do the least good and where, perhaps, a dozen others have been placed before that same day, sometimes within the hour—they move on. Congratulating themselves that they are safely out of a tight place, or comforting themselves with the thought that if a trout had been hooked it would have been lost anyway in the tangled mass, they abandon the spot—but always, I opine, with a lingering look backward. That these promising but difficult waters are prone to lure the angler into danger of hanging up solidly should make them the more interesting. When a good trout is taken from them, it is usually by a master of the craft, and no compassion need be wasted upon the fish—it has fallen into good and deserving hands.

The common practice of careless anglers is to place the fly as close to the root or snag as they can, where there is but slight chance of its being seen by the fish—at least while it is upon the surface. Naturally, if the fly be sunk to a depth which will bring it within the horizontal plane of the fish's vision, it will be seen by him more readily. But in fishing the floating fly, due allowance must be made for that portion of an imaginary circle enclosing the base of an inverted cone which will not come within view of the fish at the apex. This part will be directly over him, extending at an angle measured by the diameter of the root or snag under which he is hiding, this snag and the bank naturally being included in the calculation. To reach a fish in this position, or rather to place the fly so that it will be seen by him, an imaginary semicircle should be drawn about the spot, with a diameter equal to at least twice the known diameter of the obstacle, and the fly fished on this curved line until the circumference has been covered. Unless the angler can determine accurately the depth of the water or the submerged portion of the log, root, or whatever the obstacle may be, any allowance made over and above what appears necessary from the calculation will be to his advantage.

The down-stream part of the imaginary semicircle will prove to be the least productive, for the reason that it is difficult to interest a fish from behind, he being more concerned about happenings in front of him. Nevertheless, considerable effort should be expended upon this part of it, as there is always a possibility of the fish being nearer the angler than has been calculated. Having fished it thoroughly, the water along the upper half of it may then be covered. The edge of this segment of the semicircle should be reached from a point nearly at right angles to its tangent, the angler retiring and assuming a position at a reasonable distance from the point being assailed. The rise may be looked for in that water where the swiftest part of the current flows directly toward and against the obstruction. And, as it is advantageous to have the fly cover a great distance upon the surface, it should be dropped a foot or two farther upstream from the snag than when casting to the side of it. If the flow against the obstruction be studied there will be discovered on the edge of the current nearest the angler a spot whence the fly, being placed correctly, will be carried down to the obstacle and around it and will thus be exposed to the view of the trout without danger of drag or of "hanging up." The fly alone must travel in this part of the current, and the longer it travels in sight of the fish the greater is the likelihood of interesting him. Barring, always, the chance of error, the probability of taking the fish increases with each cast made. The situation confronting the angler who fastens to a fish in this water is a very trying one, and, if a fish so hooked is to be saved for the creel, tender methods will not avail. He must be unceremoniously bundled out and away from the dangerous spot, with every turn and crook of which he is familiar.

Aside from the fact that fishing well out from an obstacle gives a fish beneath it a more certain chance of seeing the angler's fly, the method has an additional advantage in that it lessens the risk of "hanging up" on

"Fishing well out from an obstacle gives a fish beneath it a more certain chance of seeing the angler's fly."

one of the early casts—an accident that is very apt to cut short the angler's attempt if he tries to deliver his fly in places that are difficult to reach. But the angler who is unwilling to chance the loss of a fly by placing it close to a mass of drift or overhanging branches is not over-anxious to take sizable fish, and his success is usually meagre, in proportion to the risk assumed.

Fishing the "edge of the circle" will frequently be found to be more effective than the accepted practice of searching the intricate tangles and openings, and is advocated as supplemental thereto.

A rift, properly speaking, is a shallow part of the stream where the current is quite rapid and more or less broken, and may be from ten yards in length to a mile or more. Where such water is spread from bank to bank and is very shallow, with but slight change in depth, little sport may be looked for. Random casts may bring a fish or two, but it is difficult to determine closely the positions in which trout may be; and, even if it were always possible to determine their position, the size of the fish would not induce the angler to waste much effort upon them. A strong rift of fair depth, however, probably harbours as many trout and will prove as productive to the average angler as any half dozen selected pools.

The character of these rifts changes so frequently that it would be useless to attempt to describe where trout may be found in them when the water is high. Furthermore, a cast here and there is quite as likely to fall within sight of roving fish that are not averse to travelling some distance to take the fly as a cast placed with intent to cover a particular spot. The most likely place, however, is along the side of the centre of the heaviest current, the fly being so placed that it will travel at the same speed as the leader and line, or a trifle faster.

When the stream begins to fall, instinct warns the trout that he must take up less unstable quarters. He fixes upon a permanent home, and only moves therefrom when there is another rise in the stream or during his nocturnal roamings in search of food.

In early spring, when the stream is high, trout are roaming about and may be found almost anywhere. When such conditions prevail it is not uncommon to hear anglers say that most of their fish were taken on the rifts. There are times during this season when it is more than likely that the rifts will be the only stretches that prove fruitful. When such is the case the angler, while he should never overlook the pools, should spend most of his time on the swift water.

On one occasion, while fishing a stream which empties into the Delaware, near Narrowsburg, N.Y., I walked two miles down-stream to the stretch which I had chosen for my afternoon's sport. My first cast was made close to two o'clock, and at six o'clock I had taken over twenty fish, four of which, weighing over five and one half pounds, I killed, and twice as many more of the same size I returned to the stream. I got out of the stream at about the same spot I had entered it, having fished not over one hundred yards in four hours. The fish were taken in a broken rift; it seemed as if each rock in it was the hiding-place of a good one; and, though the current was quite swift, the floating fly was taken in each case slowly and deliberately. They were, it is true, not so large as one might have hoped to get in some of the deeper pools, but fair fish, nevertheless; and, as about half of them were rainbow trout, interest in the sport did not flag for a moment.

In a short rift or run forming the connecting-link between two pools, fish from both will be found occupying it when feeding, occasionally during the day, but usually at night, at which time minnows and other small fish may be picked up. Sometimes a good fish will remain in this water, but, because of the facility afforded him for entering it from above or below, this is not often the case. While this stretch is less fruitful than another which I will try to describe, it should never be carelessly fished; and, if the instructions given in this chapter for fishing the swift are followed, the effort should not go unrewarded. Many of these short rifts are met with in a day's fishing and too often are slighted by those careless anglers who seem anxious only to have their flies upon the surface of pools. They should be given careful attention, let conditions be what they may.

There are other rifts where the current seems to be travelling at its greatest speed and where the fall is sharp and continuous. Where the decline ends abruptly a pool is formed; where it is gradual, and the force of the current is spent, it spreads, fan-like, over the formation of gravel and stones, finally flowing to one bank or the other, forming another pool or another rift. The fish occupying these longer rifts or rapids may not be the largest in the stream, but are likely to be well above the average in size and worth trying for. Along both sides of the swiftest part of the current the fly may be floated successfully. A long line is inadvisable unless the angler has mastered the difficulty of handling it under such circumstances, because it is returned very quickly. He should pick out the "oily" looking spots upon which to place the fly, because there is less likelihood of its being drenched than if it is placed in the breaking water.

Conforming to the custom among many anglers, and for lack of a better term, I include in the term "rifts" those parts of the stream which, in my opinion, are the finest of all places to fish. I refer to the stretches where great boulders, and small ones too, protruding above the surface of the water, divide the current, which flows quietly but steadily between and around them.

In many cases it will be found that the banks on either side of such stretches, while not precipitous, are higher than where they border the wider parts of the stream. The bed being narrower, the depth of water will be found greater. For these reasons such sections are chosen by trout when the stream is low. The shady part of this water, if there be any, should be approached first, particularly if the weather be bright and the water low. Each boulder, in turn, should be carefully and thoroughly searched with the fly. The first attempt may be made between any two rocks, not too widely separated, at the bottom or down-stream end of the stretch, the fly being placed directly between and a foot above them. After several casts have been made the fly may be thrown a foot or two farther up-stream but in line with the previ-

"I include in the term 'rifts' those parts of the stream which, in my opinion, are the finest of all places to fish. I refer to the stretches where great boulders, and small ones too, protruding above the surface of the water, divide the current, which flows quietly but steadily between and around them."

ous casts.

Fishing the fly between such boulders serves a double purpose. As the fish lie alongside or just above them, the fly is readily seen from either position, and if it is taken near one of them the angler is saved the necessity of fishing the others, the indications being that the fish are ready to feed and that they may be lured away from their stands. On most occasions, however, the fish will be found just above the boulder and on the shady side, and the fly, persistently delivered in that position, will attract many of them.

The angler should remember that the backwater formed by the current flowing against the up-stream side of a boulder is a favourite haunt of brown trout,

"The angler should remember that the backwater formed by the current flowing against the up-stream side of a boulder is a favourite haunt of brown trout."

and should assume that the fish in the stretch occupy such positions until some indication is given that they do not. He should so present the fly that the fish is afforded a fair view of it and is not asked to come too far to take it. Rough water should be avoided when possible; but the fly should be floated on or near the swiftest part of the current, and this will usually be found close to the boulder.

When the boulders in a stretch are irregularly scattered, the course of the current being deflected by them so that the water twists and turns to escape the obstacles in its path, each one may harbour a good fish. Not one of them should escape the attention of the angler. Even those which appear to be in shallow water are worthy of consideration and sometimes yield large fish. The eddies behind them may be fished as much as he pleases, but he should not forget that on the up-stream side the greater number of fish will be found. He should avoid haste, and also the conclusion that because a fish is not risen in one spot there is none occupying it. If by carelessness, he drives out a fish, his chance of taking one higher up in the same stretch is jeopardised.

Where the current is direct in its flow, travelling, apparently, through what might be called a lane of boulders, the fish, if feeding, may be looked for in its middle along its entire course, as well as beside and above the rocks. Beginning at the bottom, the water for a very short distance may be covered from a point directly below; but after that the casts should be made at an angle of about forty-five degrees from either side, so that the fish, which may have been under the fly and have been unmoved by it, will not see the angler or his line. A sight of the line moves fish in a way that is very distressing to the angler responsible for it.

Of similar character are those stretches where the rapid current dashes against and around the boulders in them. From a distance one of these stretches appears to be a mass of tossing water, where the dry fly might be expected to be hopelessly out of place. In such parts of the stream the fall is quite sharp, the water tumbling over a succession of diminutive falls, presenting, when viewed from below, an appearance of great turbulence. Upon close inspection, however, there will be found between the boulders miniature pools, popularly called "pockets," where the current, while strong, is not direct, a great part of its force being spent in seeking new channels.

Beginning at the bottom row of the pockets, the tail of the lowest is cast over with as short a line as may be used consistently with precision. Where the water glides swiftly over the lip of the pocket the fly should be placed above and in such position that in its course down-stream it will pass close to the boulder which is deflecting the deeper and stronger part of the current. As the fly passes the boulder it should be lifted quickly but quietly from the water. A false cast or two should be made to dry it, and then it should be placed in exactly the same position as before, this procedure being continued until a rise is effected or the angler is prompted to abandon the spot. The fly may then be advanced a short distance at a time, the longitudinal position remaining the same, until the water in a straight line up-stream between the boulder and the head of the pocket is covered. The other side should then be fished in the same manner, and this without the angler having changed his own position, which should have been assumed at the start with reference to the availability of all parts of the water.

Each pocket will present practically the same features. The depth may be greater in one, the current stronger in another, but the boulders at the head and tail should be the objective points for the angler's fly in every case. Where the depth is great or the current strong, more persistence upon the part of the angler is demanded—compensated, as a rule, by a larger fish. Where the water, with but a gentle wrinkle, slips by the boulder and does not break into a fall, the fly should be placed a yard above and directly in front of the boulder, and should not be retrieved until it has passed some distance down-stream. A fish in the dead water may often be tempted to come down after the fly, and when this happens the whole scene is enacted in plain view. There is nothing quite so exciting as this in the whole sport of angling except, perhaps, casting to and inducing a fish to rise that is lying in plain view.

Trout frequently take up stations in the backwater or eddy which is formed under and behind the miniature falls in these rapid stretches. When in this position they are inaccessible to the dry fly angler. They belong entirely to the wet fly man who is familiar enough with the habits of the fish to drop his fly above the brink of the fall, allowing it to be carried over and then under the water, so that, if it is caught in the backwater, it is presented directly to the fish, which rarely refuses to take one that comes so easily. When evening comes on, however, the dry fly angler has his opportunity. The sizable fish which select these retreats during the bright days drop downstream as darkness approaches, and, if not cruising, will be found just where the current spends itself, or under and below the little eddies to the side. These eddies should be scrutinized closely if insects are upon the water. The presence of the fish will be indicated by the rise to the flies which collect there. Should there be no insects about, the fish may be induced to rise by casting repeatedly in the quieting water.

Perhaps no water on our American streams appeals more to the average angler than a beautiful pool; and yet rarely does this water fulfill the promise it seems to hold out. That pools do contain trout, and sometimes very large ones, is true; but the fact that the fish may remain unmoved, after every artifice of the angler has been exhausted in an attempt to induce them to rise, is very discouraging. This not unusual experience may be the foundation for the belief many anglers have that the larger fish have ceased to be surface feeders and cannot be persuaded to rise to a small insect. To get one of these big fish with the floating fly the angler must have "luck"— that luck which brings him upon the stream when the fish are near the surface. Success on waters of this kind depends quite as much upon the mood of the fish as upon the skill of the angler.

If the fish are feeding, or are ready to feed, upon winged insects, they will be found in a position from

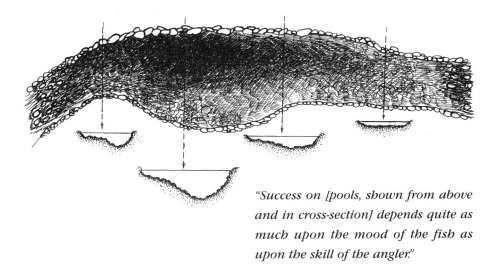

"Success on [pools, shown from above and in cross-section] depends quite as much upon the mood of the fish as upon the skill of the angler."

which the angler's fly may be seen, in which event he may hope to bring them to the artificial. But no amount of skill will induce a rise if the fish are hidden in the strongholds with which these rocky pools abound. It is absurd to expect that a big fish, lying near the bottom of a pool which may have six or eight feet of water in it, will come that distance upon the first appearance of a tiny morsel of food upon the surface. A fish that has retired to deep water is not interested in food; or, if he is, only caddis larvae, dobsons, etc., that may be picked up on the bottom, or some other sort of food considerably under the surface, will attract his attention.

Trout fortunate enough to escape the many dangers which beset them in our streams grow to great size and become largely nocturnal feeders. Night feeding is an instinct of the fish, though the smaller ones are forced by the appetite of youth to seek food in daylight, also. This is why a pool that looks as if it should contain a big fish (and probably does) yields but a few dandiprats when the condition of the water has been unchanged for any length of time. The big fish are not ravenous enough to be seeking food all of the time, and the little chaps have undisputed possession of the open water. A wonderful change in the mood of these large fish takes place when the stream is freshened after a fall of rain. The artificial fly is then taken in the most deliberate and certain manner—taken by the fish as if they knew it as a member of a family with which they have been acquainted all their lives, although it may not bear the slightest resemblance to any living insect. At such times the angler is apt to lose faith in the much-vaunted wariness and cunning of the fish and may foolishly ascribe his remarkable success to his own skill. Whether the change of water invigorates trout, or instinct tells them that they may expect food to be washed down to them, it is certain that the desire to feed is aroused, and they are at these times neither fastidious nor discriminating.

Several years ago on a stream in Sullivan County, the name of which I have promised to forget, I was in the brook just after the top of a flood and found the fish so willing that, for the particular day, at any rate, I was ready to believe the story told of some northern waters where the fish "were so numerous and so hungry that one had to hide behind a tree to bait the hook." Nearly every cast brought a slow, deliberate, businesslike rise—all large fish for so small a stream. I killed two fish that weighed one pound five ounces, and one pound nine ounces, respectively. One of these fish had two crawfish in its stomach, freshly taken; the other had a small stone catfish, pretty well digested; there was nothing else in either—not an insect of any sort. The next day was practically a repetition of the previous one—two fish killed, both just over one pound five ounces. The stomach and gullet of one were absolutely empty; the other contained a single June-bug, freshly taken, and, among a number of other insects, a waterstrider, long thought by anglers to form no part of the trout's menu. I have never been able to quite satisfy myself that this particular experience was of any great value except that it strengthened my belief that trout are moved to feed by changes in the stream caused by flood waters running down. Perhaps, also, it tended to prove that there were more big fish in the stream than I would have believed without the experience. All my fish were taken at the lips of the pools which abound in this rock-bedded stream, and I devoted my time exclusively to those places, in the hope of securing a really good fish. No small fish rose to the fly, although they are a-plenty in the stream. They had evidently been driven to other water by fear of their older brothers.

The greatest essential to success in fly fishing, wet or dry, is stream knowledge; by which I mean, not necessarily familiarity with the stream actually being fished, but that general knowledge, based on careful study of the habits of the fish, that enables the angler to select the proper part of the current in which to place the fly. Such selection is of the greatest importance when pools are being fished—it is next in importance to keeping out of sight of the trout. Under no circumstances should a pool be approached with the idea of placing the first cast in what appears to be the likeliest spot, as there is always danger of frightening the fish off if he should happen to be somewhere else in the pool. Before a fly is placed on the water, a careful study should be made of its depths and currents. If the large fish are surface feeding, they may be looked for in two places particularly: in the very lip of the pool or in the eddies at the head.

The indication that a fish is feeding at the lip or bottom of a pool is unmistakable. While the actual taking of the insect may be accomplished quietly, the fish lies sometimes so close to the surface where the water spills

It is difficult to present a fly drag-free to a trout feeding at the bottom of a pool. "A proper presentation may be made, however, and this annoying drag avoided, if the cast is so delivered that the line falls upon one of the stones or boulders which forms the lip of the pool."

out that the sharp recovery necessary in the quickening water reveals his position. This is a difficult fish to take, for the reason that, lying as he does in the shallower water—which, as a rule, has a smooth surface—he is very apt to see the angler. A long line must be used, which adds to the difficulty, as it is almost impossible to keep the line out of the swift water below the lip which snatches the fly away from the fish before he has even had a good look at it. A proper presentation may be made, however, and this annoying drag avoided, if the cast is so delivered that the line falls upon one of the stones or boulders which form the lip of the pool. The fly will then float naturally, without being pulled, until it reaches the point where the water spills out, which point it must be allowed to pass before being retrieved. If no rise is effected the cast may be repeated, and continued as long as the fish is still in position. No connection need be looked for, however, unless the fly is placed fairly close to and above the fish, and marked acceleration of pace avoided. Where there are no kindly boulders to help the angler in his deception, a chance—though a remote one—may be taken by presenting the fly in the hope that it may be taken at once, because of its accurate delivery, and before there is any drag upon it.

If, at the moment of the angler's arrival at a pool, there are no insects upon the water there will be no rise to indicate the position of a fish. But it does not follow that one is not in position and ready to feed. In this case even greater care should be exercised in approaching the lip of the pool than if a rise had been actually observed. If the angler does his work well, and has a sharp eye, the fish may often be seen lying along the side of the current as the water spills out, or just above some small boulder or other obstruction to the water's course. Sometimes the boulders may be completely under water, but their presence is denoted by a wrinkling of the surface, and the fish may be looked for just above them.

The angler must work out the problem of properly presenting the fly at each pool. In no case, however, where the fish is seen or his position is indicated by his activities should the fly be cast directly over him. It should always be cast to one side or the other, slightly above, and at an angle. This suggestion may be safely followed in every case where fish are seen and it is possible to so cast from the position occupied by the angler. When the fish are found to be occupying positions at the tail of pools—whether it be early morning, or just at dusk, or, as it sometimes happens, at midday—they are almost invariably ready to feed; and, while not always interested in insects, they are frequently induced to take the artificial because it appears close to them. Though there may have been no indication that the large fish have dropped back from the deeper water to the lip of the pool, the angler's actions should always be governed by the assumption that they are in that position until he is convinced that they are not. If he has been incautious the widening wake marking the fish's swift dart up-stream makes it quite certain that the hope of taking a trout from that particular pool must be deferred. Small fish occupying this "tail position" are as easily frightened off by sight of the angler as the large ones are, and their alarm, being communicated to the fish above, destroys whatever chance there might otherwise have been on the upper water. It is the carelessness with which the average angler overlooks this important part of the pool that is responsible for the many failures registered on what should be productive water.

It frequently happens, particularly when the water is low and bright and has not been recently disturbed, that trout are lying a few yards above the lip of the pool in the quiet water. The presence of the fish is disclosed by the wake made by him in his rush for a fly that has been presented somewhere near him. The direction the fish is taking is easily discernible, and, if he is headed down-stream—which is often the case—the situation is one that requires the gentlest possible handling. The angler should remain motionless, leaving his fly upon the water even at the risk of having the line become entangled about his feet, because the fish, being headed in the angler's direction, will be quick to detect any motion; and the rod should not be moved under any consideration. The fish, after having composed himself, will be headed up-stream again and, if not actually seen by the angler, may be assumed to be where the wake ended.

It is quite usual for a fish, after having made a rush toward the fly, to abandon the chase when the fly approaches too closely to the spill, to assume a position where he stopped, and to wait there for another insect to come down. This is the angler's opportunity; but if it is to be of any advantage to him deliberation must mark his every action. The fly must be dropped gently over the marked spot and should not be retrieved until it has passed below the rod. It will be difficult to overcome the impulse to retrieve the fly, even though it is getting farther beyond control all the time; but, as the fish has possibly been interested in it and, having turned, will immediately detect any action of the rod and be off at once, such impulse must be resisted. By stripping the line in with the disengaged hand, the fly may be recovered and presented again. Until the fly is taken by the fish, or until the angler is convinced that it will not be taken, every motion should be very deliberate. If the fish is not risen on the first cast, each succeeding throw should be made a little farther up-stream than the previous one, until the point where the fish was first seen is reached. The fly should not be retrieved in any case until it has passed over the water covered before—and it should travel in the same lane after each cast. A fish spotted as described will surely fall to the rod if the angler is careful, and his taking will afford some of the most pleasurable moments spent upon the stream.

When the angler decides to abandon the lower end of the pool, it is much wiser for him to use a longer line to reach the upper water than it is to advance up-stream, because by wading up he may frighten a fish lying in the part of the pool already covered and thus warn off the ones above. The entire pool should be carefully scanned for indications of feeding fish before any attempt is made to cast over the upper part of it. The eddies on either side of the main current at the head of the pool should be given particular attention. Should a large fish inhabit the pool the eddy will be his dining-room. He will occupy it, however, only at certain intervals, and, if the angler should be fortunate enough to arrive at a time when he is seeking food, it ought to yield a fine trout. Rarely meeting competition because of their size, the fish in these eddies are very deliberate in their feeding—securing such insects as may be on the surface with but little effort. For this reason many opportunities are missed by the unobservant angler who fails to notice the gentle wrinkling of the surface, or the small bubble left upon it, as the fish sucks in some tiny insect, and by the careless angler who sees the slight disturbance, and attributes it to a small fish. Some of the largest fish I have ever killed gave no indication of their size as the fly was taken, and not until they had fastened did I realise how heavy they were. The slightest indication of action in the eddy should be investigated thoroughly with the fly; for, while only a small fish may be taken in one, the next may produce "the big fish."

Throwing to a fish in the eddy of a pool requires some care, but a close study of the currents will make it comparatively easy. Trout always lie with heads to the current, and those in an eddy are no exception; consequently, they will be headed *down-stream*, or against the current, which is flowing *up*. This position of the fish must be taken into consideration when the fly is to be presented from below, and the angler will find that his greatest difficulty will be in keeping out of sight. How he may do this he must decide for himself, but, even at the risk of being seen, he should cast up-stream from *directly below* the fish; *i.e.,* from a position on the same side of the swift current as the eddy he is fishing. If the fly is dropped in that part of the current which is turning up-stream it will be carried to the fish in a natural manner, and if care has been taken in placing the line loosely in the comparatively dead water below, the progress of the fly will not be impeded. If the fish has been well spotted, the fly should be dropped a foot or two below him, and always in that current which will bring it directly to him. In this particular situation the first cast should be the telling one, because if the fly is not taken it is not returned to the angler immediately, and its retrieve against the current is likely to be disturbing to the fish. If the fly has been carried over and beyond the spot where the rise was seen, it does not follow that it has passed over the fish and been refused. He may be backing up under it, and may take it a yard from where he is presumed to be, if it travel that far. However, if satisfied that the fly is not going to appeal to the fish—which conclusion should not be reached until the fly is no longer in a natural position—the retrieve may be made very slowly and carefully, after which the angler may wait a minute or two, or until the fish rises again.

Sometimes the fly will be carried by the eddy toward the swift, down-stream current and be caught in it. In this event, it is easily retrieved without disturbing the water in the vicinity of the fish, and may be presented again immediately. A fish should not be given up while continuing to rise steadily; he will become accustomed to the artificial, and will take it in time, if its action is not unnatural. An eddy should be fished in the same careful manner whether a fish is seen feeding in it or not; but, in the latter case, while a fish may be in position and ready to feed, the varying currents and the difficulty encountered in attempting to retrieve the fly delicately against them destroy its natural action, and prevent, to a certain extent, proper simulation of a "hatch." The fly can cover but a short distance before it is necessary to retrieve it, and this makes for rather tedious work, because it must be brought back slowly and gently until it is out of the eddy before it is taken from the water. In this connection, it may be borne in mind that it is possible to decoy a fish from the eddy by placing the fly on the edge of the swift, down-stream current nearest the eddy, permitting it to float down three or four yards each time. If a half dozen casts have brought no response, it is better to discontinue casting than to risk driving the fish to another part of the pool, and thus disturb some other fish that might have fallen to the rod later had it remained unmolested.

CHAPTER V
THE IMITATION OF THE NATURAL INSECT

Within a very recent period, it has been asserted, upon scientific authority, that fish are colour-blind.[1] If this be true, though it is difficult for the mere angler to understand how it may be proven, the theory of those who believe that it is necessary to imitate in the artificial fly the colour of the insects upon which trout feed must be abandoned.

Writing upon the subject no longer ago than 1904, Sir Herbert Maxwell, certainly a competent observer, said: "My own experience goes to convince me that salmon, and even highly educated chalk-stream trout, are singularly indifferent to the colours of flies offered to them, taking a scarlet or blue fly as readily as one closely assimilated to the natural insect. Probably the position of the floating lure, between the fish's eye and the light, interferes with any nice discrimination of hue from reflected rays."

Cotton and the many angling writers who followed him all dwelt with insistence upon the necessity for close imitation, especially in relation to colour. In 1740 John Williamson stated the principle in the following

---

1. It has been proven with modern research that trout see color, even ultraviolet and infrared colors invisible to the human eye, quite well.

words: "... as the great Difficulty is to obtain the Colour of the *Fly* which the Fish take at the Instant of your Angling, it is impossible to give any certain Directions on that Head; because several Rivers and Soils are haunted by peculiar Sorts of Flies, and the Flies that come usually in such a Month of the Year, may the succeeding Year come almost a Month sooner or later as the Season proves colder or hotter. Tho' some Fish change their Fly once or twice in one Day, yet usually they seek not for another Sort, till they have for some Days glutted themselves with a former, which is commonly when those Flies are near Death, or ready to go out." Then, giving some simple instructions in regard to tying flies, he quotes Walton: "But to see a Fly made by an Artist is the best Instruction; after which the Angler may walk by the River, and mark what Flies fall on the Water that Day, and catch one of them, if he see the *Trouts* leap at a Fly of that Kind. . . ." Williamson's book was practically a compilation, containing the best of what had been written by anglers before him, together with his own observations.

From Williamson's time no work on fly fishing seemed complete unless instructions were given in the art of fly making, with a description of the sorts and colours of furs, silks, feathers, etc., suitable for the imitation of the natural insects held to be so necessary; but until the appearance in 1836 of Ronalds's "Fly Fishers' Entomology," it cannot be said of any author that the instructions given by him were the result of scientific study. Ronalds was most thorough in his investigation, and his experiments in regard to the senses of taste and hearing of trout are extremely interesting and instructive. While his conclusions run counter to the opinions of many other angling writers, to my mind they appear logical and are convincing; and I think he proves that trout do not have the senses of taste and hearing developed to the degree of acuteness attributed to them by other writers. Following some advice as to the choice of flies, Ronalds says: "It should never be forgotten that, let the state of weather or the water be what it may, success in fly fishing very much depends upon showing the fish a good imitation, both in colour and size, of that insect which he has recently taken; an exact resemblance of the *shape* does not seem to be quite as essential a requisite as that of colour, since the former varies according to the position of the insect either in or upon the water; but a small fly is usually employed when the water is fine, because the fish is then better enabled to detect an imitation and because the small fly is more easily imitated. The resemblance of each particular colour, etc., is not required to be so exact as in the case of a large fly." Notwithstanding his evident preference for colour over shape or form, Ronalds was careful to have the proportions of his imitations exact. The many editions of his work that have been issued, and the frequent reference made to him by later writers, is evidence that his opinions are held in high regard by anglers.

About three years before the "Fly Fishers' Entomology" appeared, Professor James Rennie, in his "Alphabet of Scientific Angling," ridiculed the theory of imitation. He says: "It is still more common, however, for anglers to use artificial baits, made in imitation or pretended imitation, of those that are natural. I have used the phrase 'pretended imitation' as strictly applicable to by far the greater number of what are called by anglers artificial flies, because these rarely indeed bear the most distant resemblance to any living fly or insect whatever, though, if exact imitation were an object, there can be little doubt that it could be accomplished much more perfectly than is ever done in any of the numerous artificial flies made by the best artists in that line of work. The fish, indeed, appear to seize an artificial fly because, when drawn by the angler along the water, it has the appearance of being a living insect, whose species is quite unimportant, as all insects are equally welcome, though the larger they are, as in the case of grasshoppers, so much the better, because they then furnish a better mouthful. The aim of the angler, accordingly, ought to be to have his artificial fly calculated, by its form and colours, to attract the notice of the fish, in which case he has a much greater chance of success than by making the greatest efforts to imitate any particular species of fly." That this statement caused considerable discussion— probably because it was made by a professor of zoology— is evidence by the appearance in 1838 of "A True Treatise of the Art of Fly-Fishing," written by those strong advocates of the imitation theory, William Shipley and Edward Fitzgibbon, who devoted a whole chapter to controverting the professor's theories, calling upon the writings of Bainbridge, Best, Taylor, Davy, Ronalds, and others in support of their opinions, concluding with the statement that "they flattered themselves that they had triumphantly done so." It seems to me that, though they argued with vigor and vehemence, they have proven nothing, conclusively, except their ability to place a construction upon the professor's statements that afforded them an opportunity for the discussion. A careful reading of Rennie shows that he merely expressed the opinion that the greatest efforts of the angler should be to make his fly one that would attract the notice of the fish by its form and colour, rather than to imitate any particular species of fly. To be sure, we have no knowledge of what his ideas with regard to form and colour were; we may assume, however, that he believed that if a red fly four inches long with yellow and blue wings and a green tail would attract the fish, such would be the fly to use. The illustration is absurd, of course; but we have a right to infer that his belief was that any form or colour which would attract the fish would do.

He advanced the theory that the trout took the artificial because they were near-sighted; apparently he did not believe that they took it because they were colour-blind.

The English creation known as the "Alexandra," representing absolutely nothing in insect life (at least to eye of man), strongly supports Professor Rennie's theory. Its effect upon trout has been so deadly that it has been suggested by many English anglers that its use would be barred upon some streams. In the same class with the Alexandra might be placed our own American nondescript, the "Parmacheene Belle," the invention of Mr. Henry P. Wells, whose theory was, "An imitation of some favourite food is in itself sufficient under all circumstances, provided it is so conspicuous as readily to be seen . . . and the fly in question was made, imitating the colour of the belly fin of the trout itself." This theory may be sound enough, but in this particular application of it one is asked to believe that the trout is inordinately fond of the belly fin of its relatives, which seems to me to be straining credulity overfar. To some old cannibalistic fish these fins may be attractive. I do not deny it, for I do not know; but in my own experience I have not known them to be plucked or bitten from the victim; nor are they found floating about loosely. The Parmacheene Belle is undoubtedly an imitation of the belly fin of a trout, but it is not an imitation of any favourite food of the fish. Its value as a lure is well known to those who fish in the lakes and streams of Canada and Maine, but trout do not take it because they recognise it as a familiar article of diet. They probably take it because of its brilliant colour, in which respect it embodies Professor Rennie's idea of what a "fly" should be. Being made up of reds and whites, it probably reflects more light than do sombre-hued patterns and, consequently, is the more easily seen. As a rule, it is taken under water, and most often after it has sunk to considerable depth.

Speaking of the Alexandra, Mr. Halford says: "It certainly is not the imitation of any indigenous insect known to entomologists; possibly the bright silver body moving through the river gives some idea of the gleam of a minnow. Long ere this its use should have been prohibited on every stream frequented by the *bona-fide* fly-fisherman, as it is a dreadful scourge to any water, scratching and frightening an immense proportion of the trout which are tempted to follow it." If this means anything, it means that trout are at first attracted by the fly or lure, but upon closer inspection discover the cheat, and, taking it uncertainly, are often slightly pricked, or, refusing it entirely, are sometimes scraped by the hook as they turn away. This criticism, it seems to me, might be directed equally well against any creation of feathers, fur, and tinsel that is fished sunk.

While rather off the main point, I may be so bold as to say that, while the sunk fly method does not appeal to me at all, I cannot readily see that it scratches many fish or frightens them in any way; and, if it did, the recollection of the affair would not linger long enough in the trout's memory to injure the chances of his being taken the next day on a dry fly, or even on another sunk one. Mr. G. E. M. Skues, who advocates the use of the sunk fly on the same streams where correct imitations are presented to rising fish, says that he presents imitations of the nymphae in the positions occupied by the naturals; that he rarely scratches a fish, and hooks but very few foul. The inference in this case might be that the trout fastens to an imitation more readily than to an Alexandra—one really deluding the fish by its natural appearance, the other exciting only its curiosity or ire.

While exhibiting an admirable filial loyalty, many of us have been prone to be governed by tradition, and the education we received in the beginning from our fathers. With few exceptions, we have trudged along the beaten path, looking rarely to right or left, but backward a great deal, using the same flies our father used before us, emulating their methods, and admiring their successes. We have overlooked the fact that we are contending with conditions that have decreased the number of native trout, and that would have taxed even the great skill with which we have endowed those of loving memory. I remember that one of my father's favourite flies was the Queen-of-the-Waters. Naturally it became one of mine, and I used it religiously—remembering its successes, forgetting its failures. A story connected with this fly may prove interesting, and perhaps tend to show how close I was to becoming a confirmed colourist, or, rather, a strong believer in the trout's ability to detect colour.

Many years ago, while preparing for a short trip to the stream, I discovered that I did not have a single Queen-of-the-Waters in my fly book. On my way to the railroad station I stopped in a tackle shop and asked for a dozen of that pattern. The clerk was unable to find any in stock, but suggested that I try a dozen called King-of-the-Waters. Although there was, in fact, little similarity between these two patterns except in the name itself, this seemed sufficient to my ignorant mind, and I took them. The following day, upon the stream, my case of three flies (I was a wet fly angler then) was never without a King-of-the-Waters—and not a fish did I take with it. I attributed my non-success to the pattern of fly, and it never occurred to me at the time that very few fish were taken at all that day, although

The classic King-of-the-Waters wet fly was the inspiration for the Pink Lady.

many anglers were on the stream. The next morning, when I opened my fly book, I found that a great deal of the red dye used upon the silk body of the fly had come off on the drying pad. The body of the fly was now a beautiful pink. Out of curiosity I wet the fly, and the pink body turned a brilliant red. I thought the thing over, and decided that I had stumbled upon an explanation of the failure of the fly to take the day before. The body of the fly originally was red and was evidently meant to appear so to the trout. When wet, however, it had turned a muddy brown. With most of the colour washed out, the fly turned a darker shade when wet, became really red, and stayed red. I determined that if this was the colour the trout wanted, they should have it, and I soaked a half dozen flies in a tumbler of water, pressing and squeezing every bit of dyestuff out of them that I could. They were all pink-bodied when I had finished with them. Recollections of the following day are still fresh in my mind. The fish seemed frantic to get my fly. I used one as the stretcher, and it was taken almost to the utter exclusion of the other patterns above. I remember that, while sitting upon a boulder in midstream tying another pink fly on in place of the hand dropper, as an experiment, I lost it in the swift current, and felt almost as badly as if I had lost a friend. The fly used as a dropper was taken readily, but not so often as when used as a stretcher, yet often enough to make me feel that I had made a great discovery. Since then, however, I have often wondered if it really were a discovery, or if, indeed, the old Queen-of-the-Waters, under the circumstances and conditions prevailing at the time, would not have been just as killing, and probably just as great a failure the preceding day.

Many years have passed, and I am still using the pink-bodied fly, modified in form, however, but never the Queen-of-the-Waters. I cannot say that I think it takes any better than the Whirling Dun or the Pale Evening Dun, which are among my favourites. Frequently, when I have found the pink-bodied fly taking well, I have changed immediately to one of the others, and have found no marked difference in their taking qualities. The pink-bodied fly in its present form—that is, tied in accordance with my own practice—has upright wings and a tail, and in appearance is not unlike the Red Spinner. It has been dubbed the "Pink Lady" by one of my friends, a name that it seems destined to carry, as it has already appeared by that name in a tackle dealer's catalogue. As to whether or not the trout is attracted by the brilliancy of the body, or by the rib of gold tinsel that gives it a fillip other flies lack, or because it bears a fairly close resemblance to the Red Spinner, I cannot venture an opinion. That it is a taking fly, however, I have demonstrated many times upon the stream. I am inclined to believe that its typical form, rather than its colour, appeals to the fish. Opposed to my opinion, however, is that of many of my friends who use it, one of whom, in particular, contending that the pink-bodied fly will take fish anywhere at any time. He firmly believes that its colour constitutes its charm. It is an interesting fact, considered in this connection, that the gentleman himself

With its early popularity the Pink Lady inspired controversy over the power of color to attract trout to the surface.

is, to some extent, colour-blind.

Objects floating upon the surface of a shallow stream reflect the colour of the bottom in varying degree, according to their density. A number of white objects floating above a moss or grass covered bottom reflect different tones of green, that one which is most opaque showing the darkest shade, and each one reflecting a lighter tone in proportion to the amount of light that filters through it. It is true, of course, that a yellow insect floating over this same bottom would reflect a shade of green all its own, and it is but natural to assume that if the same shade or tint of yellow is used in the artificial, its employment would more nearly approximate the effect of reflection upon the natural insect; but if the exact shade or tint is important, the effect is not produced unless the same amount of light passes through both natural and artificial. The use of the hook itself precludes the possibility of any delicate imitation of nature, and the infinite pains anglers have taken to make representations of the segmentations of many of the *Ephemeridae* by using quill windings for the body would seem to be for naught, except in so far as they affect the artistic eye of those using them. Many such flies undoubtedly take fish, but I dare say not because they represent particularly the *colour* of the natural.

It would seem, therefore, that the most important consideration of the fly-tier who seeks to imitate the colour of the natural insect should be the materials to be used. Consequently he should select only those which are transparent, or at least translucent, and that reflect the surroundings as readily as the natural insect does as it floats down-stream on the surface of the water. It is, of course, quite obvious that the artificial, no matter how cleverly it may be fashioned, cannot present the same appearance of translucence as the natural; but one skilfully made of the appropriate materials will approximate it nearly enough for all practical purposes. I believe that the effect produced by reflection of the colour of the bottom is not so marked upon an insect resting with its legs upon the surface and its body above it, as it is upon the insect with its body directly on the surface. If the artificial could always be cast so that it rested only upon its hackle, perhaps the difference between it and the natural would not be so marked. This may be accomplished, perhaps, by those anglers who are wedded to fishing the rise, and who keep their fly absolutely dry until a fish is seen feeding, but it is asking too much of those who enjoy seeing their fly upon the water over likely places.

Although, in certain species of insects which interest anglers, the difference in size and colour between the sexes is not great, in others it is quite marked; and some anglers are of the opinion that an imitation of the female of a species is a more killing pattern than one of the male. A most ingenious explanation of the fish's preference for the female insect was offered by the Reverend J. G. Wood in his "Insects at Home," published in 1871. He says: "Should the reader be an angler, he will recognise in the female pseudimago the 'Green Drake,' and in the perfect insect the 'Grey Drake.' The angler only cares for the female insects, because the fish prefer them, laden as they are with eggs, to the males, which have little in them but air." The statement certainly endows the trout with a fine sense of discrimination and taste. That the female insects are preferred by the trout may possibly be true, but it is to be regretted that the author did not explain how he arrived at the conclusion that they are preferred because they carry eggs. If he was an angler himself, it was probably the result of personal experience in the use of either the insect or its imitation; or autopsies upon fish may have revealed the fact. In the latter case, the discovery of a preponderating number of females in the stomach of the fish would naturally influence his opinion; but even this discovery could hardly be said to prove that the trout had a preference for the female because it was "laden with eggs." If our author did not fish for trout, his knowledge may have been based either upon information obtained from some angler or upon his own observation of feeding fish; in the latter case, being more of an entomologist than an angler, it is not unreasonable to suppose that his interest was centred upon the insect, and not upon the fish. Having seen a number of females taken in succession— probably at a time when they were predominant—the fact would indicate to his scientific mind a preference for the sex on the part of the fish.

If the fish does in fact prefer the female, the explanation may be found in the life history of the May-fly, which indicates that the male, some time after the sexual function is performed, falls lifeless, while the female, shortly after intercourse, hovers over the water, and, touching the surface with that part of her body carrying the now fertile eggs, deposits them as nature has decreed. It is this action, made in a succession of dips, the insect finally resting upon the water, which presents that appearance of life so attractive to feeding fish, trout naturally ignoring a dead insect when their attention is attracted to a fluttering one. If trout never took the male insect, nothing would be gained by imitating it; but they do—though when they do, it is generally because there are no interfering females about; or, to be more gallant, when the more attractive sex is not strongly in evidence. It naturally suggests itself to the angler that when the females of any species are predominant upon the water, it is advantageous to present a close imitation of them in colour and size—the form of the sexes being similar.

It seems to me that the colourist, as a rule, is much too certain that his flies appear to the trout as they do to his own sense of sight; surely, there is no way of demonstrating or establishing what the truth may be. Certain it is that up to the present time, it has not been possible to fashion an artificial fly that would give even a faint semblance of the translucence of the natural insect; and this, it seems to me, is a very important consideration. Using materials available, it is quite impossible to duplicate this delicate appearance of the live insect, and my own conclusion is that materials which will most nearly represent it by permitting a filtering of light are the ones to be employed—preferably materials of quiet tone and colour.

I am of the opinion, also, that the colour, or perhaps the transparency, of the wings of the artificial fly is quite as important as the colour of the body; and I am satisfied, so far as my own angling is concerned, that all erect-winged flies should be tied with wings made of feathers from the starling's wing, or flues from the inside wing feather of the mallard or black duck. For, while trout may not be able to distinguish quite so readily the colour of the wings out of the water as the body of the fly on the water, the natural appearance of the wings may prevent them from scrutinising the body too closely, and thus discovering discrepancies in its coloring; and, while wings of

"All erect-wing flies should be tied with wings made of feathers from the starling's wings."

light silvery grey may not appear so to the fish, to my eye they produce a close resemblance to the transparent, gauzy wing common to all of the *Ephemeridae*, in both the dun and perfect states.

I have a decided preference for winged flies, but that is because they look more like living insects to me when they are on the water than do hackled flies, and not because I think they appear more natural or lifelike to the fish. In practice I have found that hackled flies are taken quite as readily floating as ever they were when I fished them under water, and it may very well be that the hackle fibres standing out from and around the body on and above the surface of the water are even a better imitation of the wings of the *Ephemeridae* than are the feathers of the winged variety. Certainly a greater amount of light passes through them, and the result may be a better representation of the transparency and neuration of the wings of the natural insect than can be had from the use of artificial wings. At any rate, hackled flies float admirably, and the fish take them freely. And, although the dry fly anglers who use them may feel that something of form and appearance has been sacrificed to utility, their aesthetic sense will probably survive the shock when they find themselves successful—even those who insist that their fly be always beautifully cocked. If it is a consideration to be reckoned with, a hackled fly will outlast a dozen winged ones, being easily dried and humoured back into shape; while, on the other hand, a winged fly is almost hopelessly ruined when taken by a fish. In my own fishing I use a new fly over each fish—an extravagant habit, perhaps—but I love to see a natural looking artificial floating on the water. An old, mussed-up fly may continue to take fish as did the one fly we all have recollections of, that took fish until it was worn to a ravelling, and no other would do; nevertheless, the use of a fresh fly is good insurance against defeat, and, aside from its extravagance, the practice is recommended.

If the angler is to fish with a floating fly, the necessity of some imitation of colour and form is quite evident, but imitation need not be carried to the extent of copying minute variation of colour in slavish detail. To copy the form of the natural fly is, of course, practically impossible. The quantity of hackle used on the artificial to represent the legs of the natural (which number six at most) could hardly be lessened, so great is its aid in floating the fly. Mr. Halford recommends tying the tail of the artificial in four whisks so as to increase its buoyancy, even though the setae of the natural number but two in most cases—never more than three. The use of these parts in slightly exaggerated form does not denote a contempt for the keenness of the fish's vision on the part of the angler employing them. Rather, they are a necessary evil, and, after all, show a divergence in form in no way so marked as that occasioned by the hook.

If approximately exact imitation of form of the dun or subimago of the *Ephemeridae* is attempted, the wings of the artificial should be tied so as to stand close together and directly upright over the body. But a deviation from this form to the extent of having the wings separated will enable the angler to present the fly cocked more frequently, to drop it lightly, and will work but little harm.

In my own fishing I am willing to risk any defeat which a slight variance in colour may invite, if the fly will float erect and in the place I wish it to. While delicacy in handling the line will place the fly upright more often than not, "cocking" the fly is unfortunately not under direct control of the angler. "Cocking" is a very important part of the imitation of the natural insect—that imitation described as "position"—but it is not so essential as the accurate and delicate placing of the fly, which last depends entirely upon the skill of the angler. Perhaps "position" is best described by saying that it includes both "attitude" and "plane."

The plane in which the fly is to travel must be selected by the angler, and a combination of the judgment which prompts this selection, and the skill which maintains the plane during a great number of casts, will contribute more to success than the presentation of any particular pattern of fly. As a matter of fact, it is perhaps the only form of imitation which approximates nature—a fly sitting upon the water, being carried down-stream in the same current, and as unhampered and unrestrained in its action as a natural insect. Reliance upon certain patterns purporting to represent certain insects is never so strong again with the angler who, by his own skill, produces an imitation in this way that deludes a good fish. The governing consideration in the practice of this theory of imitation is the selection of the proper current in which to place the fly, and the angler, being guided naturally by his knowledge of the habits of the fish, should make a close study of the trend of the stream currents—particularly of those upon its surface—before beginning operations. Whether or not the fly is to be placed an inch from the bank, or a foot or two away, should depend entirely upon this observation, plane being always the important consideration.

The surface currents carry down numbers of insects, both dead and alive, and the edge of that one which is carrying most drift and is travelling slowest should be chosen by the angler for the delivery of the artificial—always with regard to the avoidance of drag. If there are no insects about or upon the surface of the water, small drift stuff, leaves, twigs, and the like will be carried down in the same plane, and under this surfaced drift the fish will probably be lying. He is interested in things upon the surface, and it is the angler's business to know it, and to so present the fly that it will come down as naturally as an unhampered insect.

It seems hardly necessary to state that it will be found well-nigh if not quite impossible to imitate the fluttering of a fly over or upon the water, by means of the rod. Yet many of us, when wet fly fishing, have deluded ourselves into the belief that, by the use of a dropper-fly and its careful manipulation, we were simulating, to a certain degree, the fluttering of the natural insect. At any rate, when the fly was taken we flattered ourselves that this was the case. Yet frequently, with the angler's attention centred upon giving to the dropper-fly a proper motion, the submerged tail-fly was taken, and usually by the larger fish. Instead of weakening one's faith in the dropper-fly and the efficacy of its jerky motion, experiences such as these have been known to strengthen a belief in the method; and I have heard the idea expressed that the action of the dropper-fly on the surface had attracted the attention of the fish to the tail-fly. This may be true, but, as a matter of fact, the sunk fly was

It is motion that attracts trout to both the sunken and the bouncing surface fly with the classic two-fly dropper rig.

115

the better imitation of life, which perhaps accounts for the fish's preference for it.

Those who practised fly fishing in the manner described paid little regard to imitation of colour, and perhaps less to imitation of form; a comparison of the ordinary tackle-shop wet fly with the natural insect will convince any doubting angler that this is so. When they did attempt to imitate the colour of the natural fly, they were accustomed to give little or no thought to colour changes likely to take place upon immersion, with the result that in many cases where silk was used upon the body of the fly, these changes were great enough to destroy almost at once any resemblance to nature the artificial might have had before it was wet. I sometimes find myself believing that these anglers, when they considered colour at all, considered it only in relation to its effect upon their own eyes, and without any regard to the fish's view of it—perhaps not entirely without reason. True, the changes in, or loss of, colour were offset to a considerable extent by the motion, more or less rapid, imparted to the fly, which prevented close scrutiny by the trout, and detection of the fraud. My own notion is that as the fly had to be taken quickly by the fish, if at all, it was taken because it was moving and might be food of some sort and not because it looked like or was an imitation of any particular insect.

There are a great many expert anglers in America who fish with accurate or close imitations of the natural insect, wet or sunk, and who, by virtue of their skill in throwing the fly and their knowledge of the haunts and habits of the trout, are enabled to basket fish of fine quality and size— fish that would be creditable to the angler's skill under almost any circumstance of capture. I hazard the opinion, however, that they derive less real sport from their method than does the angler who fishes with a single dry and floating fly, imparts no motion to it, and presents an imitation of a natural insect which the trout is at liberty to inspect and, if his suspicion is aroused by the transparency of the fraud or because of some mistake in delivery, to reject. The dry fly angler must know quite as much of the haunts and habits of the fish as the wet fly angler and, to cast his fly success-fully, must have the greater skill. Above all, the dry fly method is the more fascinating, because the angler actually sees the rise and the taking of the fly, the sense of sight as well as the sense of touch conducing to his pleasurable emotion. His imagination—and all ardent anglers have imag-ination—will immediately come into play, and he will find himself convinced that the imitation has really deceived the fish into believing that a living insect lay upon the water.

I venture to suggest the fancy that the taking of a trout with a nondescript fly of blue or red—the Parmacheene Belle, the Jenny Lind, or what-not—even though it may have been presented accurately, superbly cocked and lightly floating, can never produce in the angler's mind the feeling of satisfaction that attends him when he captures a fine fish with a fair imitation of the natural fly upon the water at the time, or with one which may be assumed to represent in colour and form a natural fly of a species which might be expected to be about at the season. True, I may seem to be stretching the point too finely, but I have expressed the fancy to some of my friends, who, after hearing me, were good enough to say, as indeed I hoped they would, "Why, the trout that took the gaudy fly was a fool fish that would have taken anything." They seemed to believe, as I do, that the angler who captures a "fool" fish attains to no honour; that "fool" fish are not the sort of fish one should covet. The fancy may be strongly characterised by many as eccentric, I know, but I am sure that it embodies the principle and spir-it of true sportsmanship.

The theory of imitation may not be justly attacked or lightly set aside because of the fact that nondescript flies frequently take fish,—sometimes after fair imitations have been refused. My own belief is that when the highly coloured nondescript is taken, success should be ascribed to the great skill of the angler and his particularly clean presentation of the fly, or to the fact that the fly was "popped" over and so close to a fish that it was seized because of its proximity.

The taking of trout with either of those two famous flies, the Gold-Ribbed Hare's Ear or the Wickham's Fancy, after fish have refused close imitations of the insects upon which they were feeding, might also be urged as an argument against the imitation theory, though against the colour part of it only, as those two patterns, while imitations, perhaps, of no individual insects, do bear a general resemblance to many, and may be said to be typical in form. It is quite possible that the bright tinsel body of the Wickham's Fancy, and the rib of gold wire or tinsel of the Hare's Ear, represent to the trout that beautiful, iridescent colouring plainly visible upon the body of many natural insects. It is also quite possible that the flashing of the tinsel, opaque though it is, produces that quality of translucence so apparent in the natural insect.

The theory that a counterpart in colour and form of the natural food of the trout is more likely to prove effective than a nondescript, is logical, beyond question, not only because the imitation is likely to delude the fish, but also because of the appeal it makes to the angler's own sense of fitness; for it is more than likely that the angler, knowing his imitation to be a correct one, will feel a confidence that will enable him to make a cleaner presentation of it, and to simulate more closely the great essentials—action and position. And yet within the experience of every angler there have been times when the very closest imitation of the insect upon which the trout were presumably feeding, presented in the best possible manner, has failed to excite any interest on the part of the fish, and when an artificial in no way resembling the natural in colour took trout quite as well as the closest imitation. On such occasions the faith of the advocate of close imitation probably received a rude shock.

Although considered out of fashion among fly fishermen of the present day, one occasionally meets an angler who still adheres to what is known as the "routine" system. The advocates of this system believe in the necessity of presenting to the fish a certain series of artificial flies in February, another series in March, and continuing a different series for each month of the season. The theory is based, of course, upon the imitation of those insects which prevail in the particular months. "Routine" anglers of the past probably had opinions as firmly fixed as those of anglers of to-day, and it is very likely that there were a few who persistently clung to the prescribed flies for May, when fishing that month, and used no others—fish or no fish.

Whatever effect the colour of the artificial fly may have upon trout, and however necessary the proper shade may be felt to be when casting to fish that are feeding upon some particular species of insect, it is quite certain that the angler cannot rely upon this form of imitation alone to take fish. In fishing with the floating fly the imitation of the form of the natural insect, in my opinion, is quite as essential as that of its colour, and frequently size will be found to be even more important than either. My own experiences have convinced me that imitation of the natural insect is absolutely necessary, and I put the forms this should take in the following order—the order of their importance:

1st—Position of the fly upon the water.

2nd—Its action.

3rd—Size of the fly.

4th—Form of the fly.

5th—Colour of the fly.

The degrees of importance which separate form, size, and colour may not be widely marked, and, while an exact imitation of the colour, size, and form of the insect which the trout are taking is undoubtedly the ideal combination, I believe that if failure results from any variation from this combination, colour is least responsible for it. I cannot go so far as to say that trout are entirely colour-blind, or that a correctly sized and shaped artificial dressed in blue would kill a fish that was taking a natural yellow dun, but I do believe that even a great divergence in the shade of colour of the artificial tied in imitation of the natural insect would make no material difference to the fish, if it were properly presented. In fact, it is my opinion that the artificial need not be yellow at all; that a fly of subdued colour—a Whirling Dun, a Silver Sedge, a Pink Lady, or any fly of similar conformation—will be accepted by the fish feeding upon a little yellow may if its presentation is clean.

We have all had experience with certain fish, or, perhaps, with many fish, on certain days when, although they appeared to be feeding, it seemed next to impossible to induce a rise. Such failures are invariably ascribed to lack of proper imitation—usually, colour. Sometimes the angler, if he be an expert fly-tier, sets about fashioning a fly which resembles the insect some particular fish is taking, and, presenting it either at that time or the next day, is delighted to find it taken readily. He is immediately a strong advocate of the theory of colour imitation, but he is sometimes uncertain that another pattern would not have served quite as well. Whether or not the pattern did the killing is really an open question.

Just above the dam in front of the Spruce Cabin Inn, at Canadensis, on the Brodhead, is a beautiful stretch of flat water where a great many fine fish may always be found. However, they are not always to be taken. Along the bank opposite the road, which at this point is but a few feet from the stream, is a heavy growth of wood. The rhododendron, which is quite thick, throws its roots out from the bank under water, and the interstices between these roots afford fine hiding-places for the fish. At the upper end of the wood, just where a field joins it, there is a deep hole which is the home of a very large trout—a fish that has sorely tried the patience of the few anglers who have attempted to take him. An overhanging tree prevents the delivery of a really effective cast from below, and this undoubtedly accounts for a great many failures. In three successive years I have raised this fish seven times (a very small proportion of the times I have tried for him), on four occasions leaving my fly with him, and not fastening solidly on the others. An old tree-stump to which the fish rushes immediately upon being hooked accounts for the smashes. The fish will not rise to a fly on coarse gut, and the fine gut will not hold him from the stump. If there ever was a trout that could convince the angler that exact—and even minute—imitation was absolutely essential, this is the one. He feeds regularly, and may be seen rising steadily for hours at a time. No amount of casting will put him down, unless clumsily done, and he will rise to a natural insect within a few inches of the artificial, time and again, ignoring the latter totally. On one occasion—the last time I tried for him—I failed so signally with all my favourite patterns, that I might have been convinced that exact imitation was necessary had it not been for the fact that the fish rose indiscriminately to many different sorts—spinners, gnats, and the smaller members of the beetle family, lady-bugs, and the like, and finally to an artificial which bore no resemblance to any of these. I could not imitate them all, and had tried faithfully with a fair imitation, in size and colour, of one species. It was all to no purpose, however, and to see him continually rising after the many attempts I had made was, to say the least, chastening. I finally decided, after watching him feed for ten minutes, to make one more attempt, and to keep casting the one pattern until he took it or was put down. I knotted on a fly known as the "Mole," which looks like an insect on the water at a distance, but very unlike one when examined closely. This fly was offered probably twenty times or more, without effect, the fish continuing to rise to the natural insects all about it. The cast which eventually raised him differed from any that I had previously made, though without intent on my part. When the fly alighted about a foot above the fish, it fell upon its side with one wing on the surface and the other in the air. Drifting down to within a few inches of the fish, it suddenly stood erect and cocked, this apparently the result of some pressure brought to bear upon the leader by the slow current. It had hardly assumed this upright position, and perhaps was still in the act of regaining its equilibrium, when it disappeared and I was fast to the fish. He added this fly to his collection, and while I sadly examined the leader to ascertain the extent of the damage done, I was not wholly discontented.

I threw a Whirling Dun to this fish one day over a hundred times without putting him down or having him evince the slightest interest in it. A few minutes later, going up-stream from him, I detached the fly from the leader, and, breaking the hook off at the bend, floated it down, and it was taken readily. Perhaps on this occasion I missed the psychological moment, and it is quite possible that the fly would have been taken if I had made one more cast, though not very probably. My own notion of it is that the pattern, when floated down with the hook broken off, had a certain naturalness which was lacking when it was attached to the leader. Either the leader itself was seen, or its restraint upon the fly destroyed its natural appearance. On the other hand, however, the difficulty in presenting the fly because of the overhanging tree may have prevented a proper presentation, though I think a great number of times it approached the fish admirably. Whatever the reason may have been, I did not rise him that day.

Perhaps the actions of another fish that I watched feeding steadily for over an hour may, while hardly offering a solution of the difficulty, present some basis for conjecture. A gentlemen who had observed him feeding the day before called my attention to the fact that a good trout occupied a little pocket about one hundred yards above the big fish which has given me so much sport, and he led me mysteriously away from the inn, and as mysteriously up the road, until we reached the spot where the fish was, when he asked me to look in the little eddy and tell him what I saw. For a moment or two I could see nothing but a little drift stuff, but very shortly a good-sized snout broke the surface, and a large bubble floated where it had appeared. While we spent ten or fifteen minutes watching the fish rise, I laid plans to get him the next day. In the morning I thought better of it, however, and planned to crawl down to the water's edge and study his actions at close range. In clambering down the steep bank I was rather clumsy, and he took fright and disappeared. Getting as close as I could to the water, I hid behind a bush and watched for the fish to return, which he did in just four minutes, timed by my watch. This in itself was interesting, as it tended to show how long the incident lingered in his memory. The eddy which he occupied was formed at the bottom of a rather swift little run by a large boulder that deflected a part of the stream toward the bank and started it up-stream again. The fish stationed himself exactly in the centre of this up-stream current, which was not very strong, and immediately began feeding. He rose three or four times a minute, sometimes oftener, according to the opportunities presented. There were very few insects in the air, but apparently a great many upon the surface of the water. I think perhaps a half dozen or so of different sorts alighted directly in the eddy, all of which the fish accounted for, but the majority of rises were to insects that were carried down-stream upon the surface, and collected in the eddy. They were of all sizes and shapes, from the tiniest *Diptera*, which interested him much, to a small dead butterfly, lying flat, which he examined closely, but declined. It was this discrimination that puzzled me. He took many apparently dead insects, and refused many. He never refused any that were alive, and size or colour or shape made no difference to him. Why some dead insects appealed to him and others did not, I cannot guess, unless, perhaps, those that appeared dead to me, did not look so to him. Every time he rose, it was with the greatest deliberation; never did he rush at the fly, and once when a particularly active dun fluttered on the surface close to him, instead of rushing for it as I expected him to do, he merely backed up under it, rising very slowly, finally sucking it in. Another thing I noticed was that he never went forward to take an insect. He went forward frequently to meet one, but always took it backing up. This manner of taking a fly is not at all unusual, as fish may frequently be seen backing under an artificial, sometimes even turning down-stream before taking it. If an insect showed the slightest activity, which many of them did in various ways, moving the body up and down, opening and closing their wings, or moving their legs, he never hesitated, but took it at once, even the tiniest. If the insect lay upon its side, he would drift with it a foot or two, sometimes taking it, frequently leaving it. On one occasion he backed under an insect in this position for a distance of about three feet, and stopped, apparently abandoning it; but the next instant he turned, took it quietly, and swam slowly back to his station. I was unable to see this insect as clearly as I wished, and I do not know that it moved at the moment it was taken, but from the manner in which the fish took the others, it seems likely that this was the case. Notwithstanding the decided preference shown by this fish for the moving or living insects, he rose and took a piece of twig about three eighths of an inch long which I flipped to him at a moment when he was unoccupied, and I found this twig in his stomach the next day, together with three spruce needles, two of which were green and one yellow. Would the presence of this drift stuff in his stomach indicate that the fish was near-sighted, or that such drift really had a place in his dietary?

I have found in the stomachs of trout many small sticks, plainly fresh, and which certainly formed no part of a caddis casing. Why they were taken is hard to say; some anglers have expressed the opinion, which may possibly be sound, that the fish are compelled to take them in the attempt to secure some poor shipwrecked insects which are using them as rafts. I prefer to believe, however, that they are mistaken by the fish for some form of life, perhaps having the appearance of caddis larvae. The spruce needles were probably mistaken for willow flies, or some of the family of *Perlidae*—those with wings that fold along the back.

That the fish was taken the following morning on the Mole, which certainly imitated no insect with which he may have been familiar, perhaps means nothing. As he was feeding regularly, and rather indiscriminately, he was probably an easy fish to take. The Mole was just another morsel that looked natural enough. The first cast took him, the fly drifting up to him after having been cast over the boulder at the bottom of the eddy. The leader was not seen, and as the fly appeared in a natural, upright position, his suspicion was not aroused, and a minute or two later he was in the net. Withal, the fish showed a decided preference for living insects, and refused those which were certainly no deader than an artificial fly; and yet the Mole was taken with just as much confidence as if it had been a living thing. I think it quite within reason that any pattern of fly properly presented would have taken the fish as readily as did the fly which he rose to, and my conclusion is that it was because of its position that it was taken. My observation of this fish confirmed my belief in the necessity of so placing the fly that it would come to the fish just as a natural insect would, floating upon the surface. There is a great difference between the effect produced by a fly cast upon likely looking water, or to a feeding fish, without special care as to where it may alight, and that produced by one cast exactly to the proper spot.

The larger fish down-stream apparently was interested only in live insects, which is shown, I think, by his utter refusal of every artificial of any pattern, including the Mole, which he ignored each time it came over him, until the twist in the leader, or some other uncontrolled action, turned the fly over on the surface, and simulated to a certain extent the struggle of an insect endeavoring to rise from the water. I am convinced that my many failures with this fish were due, in the main, to my inability to place the fly in a proper position. This conclusion is supported, I think, by the fact that he took the unattached Whirling Dun—which I was careful to float down to him in the proper current—after he had refused it scores of times when attached to the leader.

CHAPTER VI
SOME FANCIES—SOME FACTS

Some anglers have come to believe that the trout of our heavily fished streams have developed such wariness and cunning that they view the artificial fly of the angler with suspicion, even if they do not actually know it to be an imitation. In the light of certain experiences of my own, I am unable to concur in the conclusion reached by these anglers that trout are capable of reasoning or remembering specific incidents for any long period of time; it is my opinion—presented, however, with some hesitancy—that they refuse the artificial fly not because they have had previous experience with it but because of various other reasons, the most important of which are the unnatural *action* of the fly and the probability of the fish having seen the angler, his rod, the leader, or the shadow of one or all. Surely the trout of these streams cannot in July and August remember the hordes of anglers that invaded their haunts in May. Admitting it to be true that in the earlier months of the season it is comparatively easy to take trout, even when the streams are full of anglers, and that later, in the summer months, with but two or three anglers, or at most a half dozen, to be seen, infinite skill is often required to induce even a single fair rise, something other than the memory of the fish must be the cause of his reluctance to rise, as the following instances may tend to prove.

In July, 1911, I rose, hooked, and returned to the water four fish three times each in one week; and these fish were taken in the same place and on the same pattern of fly each time. On another occasion I rose and landed an eleven-inch rainbow trout which I returned to the water, and the next day this fish was brought home by a fellow angler who had taken him in the same place. This last may possibly have been another fish; but about the four other trout there can be no mistake, as I marked them without injury before returning them to the water the first time. I was prompted to make this experiment after taking a fish from one spot, which resembled closely in size and form a fish I had returned to the water a few days previously. This fish was one of the four, and was twice taken and returned. Each of the fish gave up a minute piece of its caudal fin in return for its life.

Often, too, one hears of trout being taken with the fly of some luckless or careless angler fast in its jaw. On the Brodhead, in 1907, one morning about eight o'clock, I rose and killed a native trout weighing about a pound, which had a fly in its lip left there by an angler the evening before; his nose was raw and bleeding where he had scraped it against the stones in his efforts to dislodge the hook. Experiences of this sort do not tend to confirm the belief that fish have memory.

The more enemies an animal has the more wary it is, and in those least able to defend themselves against attack the senses which enable them to avoid danger are most keen. In some animals, sight, smell, and hearing are all keenly alert; in others a combination of two of these senses is relied upon, and in rare cases but one. These faculties give warning of the approach of an enemy, and time, in most cases, for the use of such secondary means of defense as are provided by nature—speed, flight, protective colouring, or whatever they may be.

In the case of trout, since scientists have come to no definite conclusion that fish can smell, we may safely assume—from the fly fisher's standpoint, at any rate—that this sense has no place in our study. The same may be said of taste and feeling; the luckless fish relying upon these senses would find himself hard and fast before he could reach the conclusion that the feathered fly was not what it appeared to be. This leaves sight and hearing as the means by which the trout is apprised of the approach of danger—and the angler may well say that they are quite sufficient.

> "If fish could hear as *well* as see,
> Never a fisher would there be."

The experiments made by Ronalds and described in his "Fly Fishers' Entomology" prove more or less conclusively that trout cannot hear, or at least are not disturbed by sounds produced in the air. Now, while it is quite certain that they are affected by vibrations communicated to the water, the bottom of the stream, or its banks, I do not believe that the disturbance is conveyed to the senses of the fish unless the vibrations take place close to it. In this connection, an experiment made by myself may prove interesting, even though it may be in no way conclusive, as it was tried but once, and the trout which served as the medium may have been "deaf." Taking my position on a high bank above the fish and completely out of sight, I had a young man go below and thirty feet down-stream. Lying prone upon the opposite shore, which was level with the water, and taking pains not to make any quick move which might have spoiled the experiment, he took two stones, one in each hand, and, at a signal from me, struck them together, a foot under water. He did this a dozen times, each succeeding blow being harder than the previous one. The sound produced by the clashing stones had no apparent effect upon the fish, but I noticed that the series of small waves or ripples created by the disturbance of the surface, upon reaching the trout, seemed to make it uneasy, and it began "weaving" from side to side, covering, however, not more than a foot in its movements. When the fish had quieted down, and after another trial, with the same effect, I had the lad abandon the stones and make as large a wave as he could, directed toward the fish. There was considerable splashing during the attempt, but the trout gave no indication that it was aware of the disturbance until the first ripple was passing over it, when it became as uneasy as before, and even more excited; and not until the ripple had ceased did it resume the almost stationary position previously held. The fish was about one foot from the surface, and the largest ripple not over two inches in height; consequently, its motion could hardly have been felt at a depth greater than six inches; yet the fish was disturbed—whether by the action of the water itself or by the shadow cast by the ripple, I leave for the reader to decide. Of one thing I am positive: the fish was not disturbed by the sound of the colliding stones.

The fish's sense of sight is so keen that it alone enables the trout to avoid danger, and is absolutely necessary to its existence. But it is not so keen, in my opinion, as to enable the trout to detect minute differences between the angler's fly and the natural insect—except, of course, when the action of the artificial fly is so unnatural as to warn the fish, or frighten it.

Adherents to the theory that trout are able to distinguish between the angler's artificial fly and the natural insect, make much of the admitted fact that a fish is rarely taken from the much fished Southern streams on a Parmacheene Belle or other nondescript. There is a great deal of truth in the contention; but the fact is lost sight of that these flies are usually presented by anglers who have but little knowledge of the habits of the fish they are seeking, their experience having been gained solely at the expense of the trout of the wilderness.

While not asserting the opinion that a gaudy fly will not take fish, I would remind the reader that such a fly is usually cast by a man who presents himself to the fish before he offers the fly—with the inevitable result. The instinct of self-preservation is strong in the trout, and he flees the apparition, though, if he would but realise it, he was never safer than at the very moment of its appearance.

Anything unusual that comes within the vision of the fish means to him a possible danger, and the desire to feed, if he be in the mood, is forgotten in his effort to locate the point of attack. Any shadow thrown upon the water indicates the approach of an enemy—a heron, a kingfisher, a mink (the most destructive of all), or a man, in whom he recognises an enemy only because he sees a moving object. Beset as the trout is at all times, it is but natural that he should make use of his only means of defence—speed—and escape while he may. On streams that are much fished, frequent sight of man is afforded the fish, and, although the actions of the angler (except in rare cases) do not indicate the danger of actual personal encounter, the fish retires, precipitately or quietly, according to the manner in which he is approached. It is this sight of man or his shadow, and not the ability to detect the fraud, that impels him to refrain from taking the fly. If the angler remain hidden from view, and throw the fly properly, without the accompaniment of shadows of himself, rod, line, or leader, and a rise is not induced, he may safely assume that it is lack of inclination on the part of the fish, and not a contempt for the pattern of the fly, bred of familiarity with it, that causes him to refuse it.

These facts, or fancies, as they may be considered, are

131

presented only as they may support a theory that accounts for the wariness and cunning of the trout of much fished streams, and the apparent lack of these attributes in the trout of the wilderness. It is a well known fact that a man who wishes to take trout in Maine, Quebec, New Brunswick, Nova Scotia, or, in fact, anywhere in the North Wood where they are plentiful, need have had no previous experience to enable him to catch all that the law, or his conscience permits. This same man fishing in Pennsylvania or lower New York, practising the same methods he applied in the North, will leave the streams with the idea firmly fixed in his mind that they are barren of fish, or, perchance, viewing the catch made by a more skilful angler, will come to the conclusion that the fish are more wary than their fellows of the North, and that a skill unknown to the angler lacking experience on these waters is required to take them. The instinct of self-preservation is quite as strong in the trout of the wilderness, but expresses itself in other ways that are in keeping with the different conditions they have to contend with.

In most places where trout are plentiful, there is abundance of room for them to escape from an enemy, an advantage denied the trout which are restricted to the narrow confines of one of our mountain streams, particularly when the water is low and the trout have to be more wary than ever, if they are to survive. While endowed with the same agility and the same keenness of sight, the wilderness fish are emboldened by numbers, and appear to depend a great deal upon one another for warning; they are alert only to the "main chance"; *i.e.*, the taking of anything that looks like food. This explains why it is easy for the veriest tyro fishing in the wilderness to take as many fish with the fly in a single day as the expert on the Southern streams would be content to take in a season. Many of these big catches are made upon lakes and streams that are heavily fished, yet the angler rarely has to resort to methods which require any great skill. In many instances the fishing is done from a canoe, and fish are taken quite close to it, the interest on the part of the trout seemingly being actuated by nothing more than a desire to "beat his fellows to it."

The law of "the survival of the fittest" applies equally to the fish of the Southern streams and to the fish of the wilderness. In both cases vigilance and agility are the price of continued existence—on the one hand, to avoid the attack which may deprive the fish of life, on the other, to excel in the scramble for that which will sustain it.

If the old saw which runs, "When the wind is in the north the skilful fisherman goes not forth," etc., referred to fly fishing, it was plainly meant for the angler who did not care to indulge in his sport when the chilling blasts from this quarter were howling about the stream, because it is in no sense descriptive of the effect of the wind upon the feeding of the fish. When an angler has taken trout under conditions ranging from flat calms to gales from every point of the compass, it is difficult for him to believe that wind has any direct effect upon the fish, aside, perhaps, from the influence it exerts in promoting or retarding the development of the insects upon which they feed; and this last depends more upon the temperature of the wind than it does upon its force or the quarter from which it comes.

The angler who is fishing the flat, still water of a pond or lake hopes for a breeze in order that he may take advantage of the ripple caused by it, and deceive or approach his fish more readily. The advantage afforded by the breeze is offset on many occasions, in proportion to the force of the wind, by the increased difficulty of casting; and when a stiff wind is blowing down-stream or in the face of the angler it is of negligible value. So far as comfort is concerned, a chilling wind is very disagreeable, and the angler unfortunate enough to be upon the stream during a "norther" in the early spring is quite of the mind that trout are sensible of it, when he finds them in no keener mood for the sport than he is; yet it was just such a day, as cold and blustering as I have ever experienced, that the trout on the Brodhead, of which I have told, rose to the fly which was made to play such pranks by the wind.

There is a gentleman of my acquaintance, an expert with the fly, who holds that it is useless to fish a wooded stream when the wind is blowing heavily, not so much because of any change in atmospheric conditions, but because the rapidly moving shadows thrown upon the water by the frantically waving overhead limbs and branches seem to make the trout restless or nervous, and unwilling to feed. Be this as it may, it certainly does not apply upon the open stretches, for there the wind is of distinct advantage, because the ruffled surface helps to conceal the angler's activities from the fish. When success does not attend the caster's efforts on days of this sort, failure must be ascribed to his state of mind rather than to the condition of the weather.

And here just a hint from my own experience: beware of fishing in big woods on a very windy day; dead limbs may come crashing down at any moment. On one occasion a difference of ten feet in my position would have meant disaster and these pages might never have been written.

During periods of high wind the trout are often treated to a change of diet, land flies, grasshoppers, and beetles, unhappily overcome, being readily and cheerfully accepted. On one occasion, all the trout killed by five or six anglers disclosed the fact, upon autopsy, that potato-bugs had formed a large part of their food that morning; and a fly which resembled this beetle only in size and shape was found very effective. This fly was a herl-bodied brown palmer, called the Marlow Buzz.

The many anglers who still hold to the belief that trout will not rise during a thunder-storm do so, no doubt, because if offers an excuse for retiring from the stream and seeking shelter,—for which they cannot be blamed. It is not the pleasantest situation to be caught in one of the vicious storms which sometimes break with scant warning. If, however, it happens that the angler is so placed that he is far from a road or path that will lead him to some cover, he is far safer in the stream than in the woods; and, making the best of a bad bargain, he should continue his fishing. In all likelihood, he will come to the conclusion that the theory is not founded upon fact; for, while trout do not invariably rise during thunder-storms, they may be taken on occasions when the reverberations are so heavy as to be felt almost as distinctly as they are heard—the effect upon the fish not being apparent.

If the storm be accompanied by a heavy rain, dry fly fishing ceases as soon as the water begins to rise and becomes discoloured, because, even though the fish may be ready to feed, there is small likelihood of the angler's fly being seen by them through the discoloured water. But no time should be wasted in returning to the stream after the flood has run off and the water is clearing, as the opportunity for taking fish is then probably the best that will be presented.

Idiosyncrasy—or shall we call it superstition?—seems to enter into the make-up of a great many anglers.

Squire Jake Price, now dead, father of the boys who keep that comfortable hostelry on the Brodhead, at Canadensis, in Pennsylvania, well known to many anglers, was famous as a trout fisherman. He fished with the fly only, tied his own flies, and from the time his sons were able to wade the streams would permit them to use nothing else. Always keen to be at his fishing, he would not be dragged to the waterside unless his "almanac" told him the time was propitious. Curiously enough, when he did go, he always took fish; but this may be ascribed to the fact that he "knew how" rather than to a revelation from the zodiac.

A story is told of an angler of indifferent skill, but anxious to take home a basket of fish, who induced Squire Jake to accompany him one morning. He felt certain of getting trout, the Squire having approved of the day. Upon their arrival at the stream-side he proceeded to line his creel with fine grasses and ferns, when, to his amazement, the Squire left abruptly, saying he could not fish with one who would thus "fly in the face of Providence." Was this superstition, or only anger at the other's assurance?

Of similar mind to the Squire are those anglers who persist in carrying, to their own inconvenience, a diminutive creel and smaller net, preferring to cram into either a fish twice too large rather than to carry equipment of adequate size; the taking of a good fish is a circumstance which they feel may never be realised if they anticipate it.

Some consideration must be given to the belief of those who have unbounded faith in a particular pattern of fly. There are wet fly fishermen on the Beaverkill who never make up their cast of three flies without including the Royal Coachman; and at least one of these, whom I know, uses this fly, dry, in preference to any other. While the pattern has no place in my book, I respect the faith others have in it, which faith, however, is often rudely shaken—for a short period, at least. After fishing carefully for hours with his favourite fly without response, the angler meets a brother angler who displays two or three nice fish taken on the Queen, the Bumble, or what not, and passes on. For the nonce the favourite is discarded, the Queen or Bumble is knotted on, but the result is the same—nothing. Another pattern is tried—same result. Again the fly is changed, and again, and still again. In his anxiety our friend uses little skill, less judgment, and lacks entirely the great essential—faith.

Many times an angler, stepping quietly into the stream at the beginning of his day's sport, casts his fly to a spot where his experience tells him a trout may be, and meets with response almost immediately. His next cast is accepted quite as quickly, and in these few delicious moments, with the nucleus in his creel, the vision he has had of the one great day's catch begins to take tangible form. But how rudely the vision is dissipated in the next four or five hours, during which time he gets not a single rise!

There are other anglers in whom entirely different emotions are aroused when they are successful in taking fish soon after their arrival at the stream. To them this incident spells utter failure for the rest of the day. It seems to me that these men neglect to analyse the situation, permitting superstition to run riot with reason, and, to my mind, their troubles may be ascribed to any one of three causes: (1) At the time the angler first steps into the stream he may be arriving at the top or at the end of a rise that started fifteen, twenty, or thirty minutes before, which short space of time may be responsible for the difference between two fish and a possible half dozen. If the angler meets with this experience during the season when the water is very low and clear, and the day hot and bright, he may be satisfied that, to a great extent, such is the explanation. But, if he is not a principal to cause number two, he should be able to continue taking some trout, even under these trying conditions. (2) The optimist arriving at the stream side prepares his rod, surveys the scene of action, and, having selected the spot he is to fish, enters the stream some distance below, and quietly proceeds to his point of vantage. Every instinct alert, he is careful to make no mistake, and his care and deftness are at once rewarded. Continuing a few yards, another fish is taken, and possibly a bit farther on, still another. Then, blinded by conceit, he falls into the pit he has dug for himself. He thinks he has at last the right medicine, and unknowingly (and unmeaningly, bless his heart) there steals over him a feeling akin to contempt for the wary fish he is after. The next pool is approached with a swagger that fills the trout that inhabit it with consternation, and drives all thought of feeding from them. Some day it will occur to this angler that he has been a bit overconfident, and he will try getting out of the stream, going up a hundred yards through the brush, and starting all over as at the beginning; then he will come to a realisation of the truth. (3) The pessimist, by analysing cause number two, may overcome, to a certain extent, the deep-rooted superstition that, because he gets a trout easily at the outset, he will get no more throughout the day. His is a state of mind that surely is not conducive to best effort. After taking a fish on the first few casts, his subsequent proceedings are governed by an anomalous condition of mind—he believes that his sport is over, yet hopes the day may prove the fallacy of this theory, and, in an unconscious effort to avoid his fate, he fishes in a careless manner.

The rise which indicates that a large fish is feeding has, upon the minds of some anglers, a psychological effect which works toward defeating any attempt they make in throwing to him. The angler is alert only to the necessity of placing his fly near the fish, and, caution thrown to the winds, he approaches in a manner which might be called stealthy if he used it in escaping from a burning building. Having begun without cautioning, thus preparing the way to dismal failure, he fixes his eye upon the spot where the rise was noted, and sends his fly, with no thought, perhaps, other than to get it on the water as quickly as possible. If his efforts meet with no reward—and the chances are they will not—and many fish are to be seen feeding all about, he probably becomes frantic with desire to take one, runs through a rapid change of flies in the hope of finding one that will entice, wastes many precious minutes in his fumbling uncertainty, when suddenly all rising ceases, and he has lost his opportunity.

The remedy for all of these cases is the same—calmness and deliberation.

The suggestion that the sight of the leader is abhorrent to trout brings up a point upon which great stress is laid by dry fly anglers. That the fish is warned off by seeing the gut upon the surface of low, clear water is to my mind more certain than anything else in the sport of angling. Whether or not frequent sight of the leader makes the fish familiar with it, is difficult to determine. Personally, I believe that when a fish refuses a fly because he has seen the leader attached to it, his timidity is likely to be due to the impression of its unnaturalness at the moment, rather than to his recollection of having seen a like object before and learned its danger. In plain words— probably inviting a storm of protest and criticism—I am not inclined to the notion that trout become "educated" on streams that are much fished. These trout are quite sensitive to danger, but, in my opinion, only imminent danger affects them. The sudden appearance of an angler waving a rod, or of a cow fording the stream, are disturbing to trout, one just as much as the other. Both angler and cow are in motion, and that alone attracts the eye of the fish; both intercept light, and thus cast shadows upon the water, which mean possible danger to him.

Anything falling upon the surface of the water arouses interest on the part of a fish observing it; if it be a shadow, he suspects danger in proportion to its size and activity; the fall of a leaf, a twig, or an insect is interesting to him in one way or another. Frequently a leaf or twig, if not so large as to frighten him at once, will be investigated at close range. I have thrown maple buds to trout, which were taken almost immediately upon striking the water, being slowly ejected afterward when it was discovered that the buds were not food.

An insect intercepts light, but the insignificant shadow it casts does not alarm the fish, and his attention is directed to the insect alone. When the artificial fly is thrown, however, it must necessarily be with the leader attached, and if it so happens that the leader, or that part of it close to the fly, *floats upon the surface*, the attention of the fish is divided between the fly itself and the leader, the latter standing out boldly between the eye of the fish and the background of sky. The leader floating upon the surface is more visible to the fish than when fully submerged. The angler who wishes to demonstrate this may do so by placing a length of gut upon the surface of some still, sunlit water, noting the shadow cast by it upon the bed of the stream, and then comparing it with the shadow of the same gut submerged.

The water-strider, skipping nimbly over the surface of clear, shallow water, affords an excellent illustration of shadow effects. The shadows thrown upon the bottom by this curious insect are enormous when compared with its actual size, and those resulting from the depression in the surface made by the insect's feet look to be as big as a dime. It was observation of the shadows thrown by the water-strider that prompted me to experiment with the leader; and my first attempt, made with the lightest leader I had, produced a shadow upon the bottom *nearly an inch in width*. Whether or not this shadow alarms the fish more than does the leader itself, probably depends upon the circumstances controlling the direction of his attention at the time, but it is certain that one or the other does have a marked effect upon his behaviour. Perhaps both combined have, and, consequently, he can hardly be expected to take the fly when his interest is divided betwixt the desire to feed, on the one hand, and suspicion tinged with fear on the other.

Upon glassy water, the glistening leader, twisting and turning upon the surface, accompanied by little wrinkles along its entire length, presents to the fish an aspect which must at least arouse his curiosity and distract his attention from the fly—even though it does not terrify him and scare him off entirely.

The visibility of the leader has always been one of the problems of the fly fisher, irrespective of the question of drag. Many attempts have been made to produce a leader of neutral colour that would be invisible, or approximately so, when on the water. I have done some experimenting in this direction myself. I have tried all colours—greens and browns, mist colours and greys. I have steeped leaders in ink until they came out absolutely black. Yet, withal, I have failed to satisfy myself that one was better than the others, when I came to use it on the stream. If there is one colour that a leader may be stained to render it less visible than another, I do not know what it is. I am inclined to believe, however, that gut of natural colour is less conspicuous than gut that has been coloured to make it harmonise with the water. Partial solutions of the problem may be had by assuming certain controlling conditions to exist. For instance, as the fish views the leader from below, and against a background formed by the sky, a light-blue leader to harmonise with the background on a bright day, or, for a similar reason, a grey one on a cloudy day, may be the very thing. Of course, it is all very speculative, because the main element of the problem—what the fish thinks—is an unknown one.

In my opinion, the floating, drifting leader, with its wrinkles and its convolutions, constitutes the worst possi-

"The angler should endeavor to have the fly float and the leader sink—obviously, by keeping one dry and the other wet."

ble form of "drag," which must be avoided if trout are to be taken where the water is slow and unruffled. The angler should endeavour to have the fly float and the leader sink—obviously, by keeping one *dry* and the other *wet*. He will find it even more difficult to keep the leader wet than to keep the fly dry; even when thoroughly saturated, the former will not submerge readily when the fly is thrown as lightly as it should be.[1]

In swifter water it is easier to keep the leader under the surface, but here one encounters another form of drag which, while in my opinion not so fatal to the angler's chances as the one I have described, is oftentimes more exasperating. This form of drag takes place when the fly, although accurately and lightly placed in the desired spot, is snatched away almost at once by the current pulling on the line or leader; the fish may thus be deprived of an opportunity of securing the fly, or he may refuse it because of its unnatural action. The natural insect, unhampered by any "string to it," drifts naturally with the current, and the feeding fish which makes for it, having accurately judged its position and pace, rarely misses. The artificial, when drag is exerted upon it, dashes down-stream at a

---

1. Modern nylon leaders are actually harder to sink than gut leaders, which absorb water readily. The angler should rub at least the last twelve inches of his nylon tippet with a sinking agent.

speed always greater than that of the current in which it is; besides the unnatural action it acquires, it sometimes ceases to be a floating fly, being dragged under the surface by the pull of the line or leader in the swifter water. Drag of this sort usually occurs when the line or the leader must fall on the swift water between the angler and the spot he desires to reach with the fly, and is not always avoidable. Where possible, the line and leader should be kept out of the swift water.

When casting to the eddies at the head of a pool, the angler should assume a position on the same side of the current as the eddy to be fished. An effort should be made to place the line in the water that is turning *up-stream* where the eddy begins to take form. The fly falling farther up will remain floating for a time—quite long enough to be taken by a fish. If this eddy cannot be reached from directly below, because of the depth of water or on account of some obstacle to clean casting, the fly may be thrown across the current with the up-stream curve in the leader. Where this is found necessary the leader should be watched carefully and, before it begins to exert a pull on the fly, the latter should be retrieved quickly. The fly may be taken from the water quietly, as it should be, if a forward loop is thrown in the line similar to that used in the switch cast. This action removes the leader from the water with but little distur-bance, and, as the fly is about to leave the surface, the backward cast will carry it clear, practically without com-motion. In the same manner an eddy across stream may be fished with little danger of a fish being put down by the sight of a dragging fly. The method, however, calls for keen alertness, and the angler must have perfect and con-stant control of rod and line.

Swift water in either a rift or a run should have no ter-rors for the angler who fears a dragging fly, if he will first study the currents. Even if he feels that a fish is occupying water that can be reached only by risking drag, he must always bear in mind that a fish is more likely to come some distance to a natural-looking fly than it is to take an unnatural one close to it. A spot should be selected as close to the assumed position of the fish as possible; but this choice should always be guided by the necessity for placing the fly on water swifter than that in which the line and leader will fall. The "retarded" drag which may set in after the fly has been placed in swift water, has floated down-stream until it is below the leader, and is held back by it, need not be feared, because the fly will have covered a considerable stretch in its travel, and may then be retrieved. Sometimes the sight of a dragging fly is more offensive to the angler than it is to the fish; and there are occasions when it will be taken, if its actions have not been particularly rude.

As an aid to keeping the line afloat in swift water, an application of deer's fat, or one of the many preparations now made for the same purpose, is recommended. It is sufficient to treat three or four yards at the end of the line, and the dressing should be rubbed down smoothly afterward. Under no circumstances should any dressing be applied to the leader, because, even though it helps to float the fly, the gut will be found to be annoyingly buoyant when the still reaches are being fished, and will produce that troublesome form of drag already described, and which I consider the only form that unduly taxes the ingenuity and patience of the expert and even-tempered. My own opinion is that the sight of the leader does not seriously deter the fish from taking the fly in swift water. But on smooth water a superbuoyant leader is a nuisance and a plague and an abomination.

CHAPTER VII
THE POINT OF VIEW

The capture of a splendid ouananiche under circumstances most trying is somewhere described by a well-known writer, who, in his inimitable style, exhibits himself before his readers running through his entire assortment of artificial flies, first one and then another and still another, and all without avail. We see him casting, casting, all impatience, determined, perhaps exasperated. Surely some sort of lure is predicated. But what? Ah, he has it! A live grasshopper. Then follows the pursuit, the overtaking, and the capture of the grasshopper, the impaling of its unfortunate body, its proffer to the fish, a desperate battle, and, finally, the contemplation of the finest fish of the season safely landed. The thrilling moment! Which was it? Why, of all moments, that one in which he captured the grasshopper! The story affords a fine illustration of what I call the "point of view," but until after the revelation that came to me with my first success with the dry fly, I did not fully appreciate its finer and deeper meanings.

Certain pleasurable excitement always attends the taking of a good fish by the true angler. Yet, after all, the quality of his gratification should be measured by the method of capture. In angling, as in all other arts, one's taste and discrimination develop in proportion to his opportunity to see, study, and admire the work of greater artists. Even as a knowledge of the better forms of music leads, eventually, to a distaste for the poorer sorts, and as familiarity with the work of great painters leads to disgust with the chromolithograph-like productions of the dauber, so, too, does a knowledge of the higher and more refined sorts of angling lead just as surely to the ultimate abandonment of the grosser methods. One who has learned to cast the fly seldom if ever returns to the days when he was content to sit upon the bank, or the string-piece of a pier, dangling his legs overboard while he watched his cork bobbing up and down, indicating by its motions what might be happening to the bunch of worms at the hook end of the line; and, even as casting the fly leads to the abandonment of the use of bait, so, too, does the dry fly lead to the abandonment of the wet or sunk fly. There can be no question but that the stalking of a rising trout bears to the sport of angling the same relation to its grosser forms as the execution of a symphony bears to the blaring of the local brass band. It appeals to the higher and more aesthetic qualities of the mind, and dignifies the pot-hunter's business into an art of the highest and finest character.

I am thus brought to the consideration of the pot-hunter and the fish hog. Many angling writers there be who have not hesitated, nor have they been ashamed, to describe the taking of great numbers of trout on separate and many occasions. They feel, no doubt, that such narratives entitle them to consideration as authorities on the subject. I quote from one—who shall be nameless—his bragging description of a perfect slaughter of fish. After telling of twenty-five or thirty trout taken during midday, naming at least a dozen flies he had found *killing*, he concludes: "All my trout were taken from the hook and *thrown twenty-five* feet to shore. Thirty, my friend claimed, yet when I came to count tails I found *forty* as handsome trout as ever man wished to see, and all caught from six in the evening until dark, about seven forty-five. I had no net or creel, therefore had to lead my trout into my hand. The friend at whose house I was staying claims I lost more than I caught by having them flounder off the hook *while trying to take them by the gills and by flinging them ashore.*" The italics are mine. And this fellow had the temerity to add that some poor devil (an itinerant parson, he called him) annoyed him by wading in and fishing with a "stick cut from the forest." Had Washington Irving witnessed this fellow's fishing I doubt that he would have been moved to write: "There is certainly something in angling that tends to produce a gentleness of spirit and a pure serenity of mind."

There are men calling themselves anglers!—save the mark—who limit the number of fish to the capacity of creel and pockets, and to whom size means merely compliance with the law—a wicked law, at that, which permits the taking of immature trout. It is not an inspiring sight to see a valiant angler doing battle with a six-inch trout, and, after brutally subjecting it to capture, carefully measuring it on the butt of his rod which he has marked for the purpose, stretching it, if necessary, to meet the law's requirements, and in some cases, if it does not come up to the legal standard, rudely flinging it away in disgust—to die as a result of its mishandling. Happily, this tribe is not increasing, because of the persistent efforts of true sportsmen who do not hesitate to denounce it publicly whenever opportunity arises. Perhaps it is permissible to hope that the pot-hunter and the fish hog may in time disappear, but, if this desirable end is to be brought about, true sportsmen must not shun their duty but must wage unceasing war against them.

Books on angling abound in word-pictures descriptive of the strenuous battle of the hooked fish to escape its captor, many such pictures being so vividly drawn that the reader fairly imagines himself in the writer's waders, his excitement ending only when the captive is in the net. It is meet, therefore, that some consideration be given to the point of view of those anglers who believe that great merit attaches to him who lands a good fish on light tackle.

There can be no question of the excitement attending the playing of a good trout nor of the skill required in its handling, and this excitement, in proportion to the ideas of the individual, is a greater or less measure of the sport; but, given the opportunity, it is my opinion that, in the hands of a skilful angler, the rod will kill nine out of ten fish hooked. Be that as it may, can the degree of skill, even with the lightest tackle, displayed in the landing of a two or three pound trout (a fine fish on our Eastern streams) bear comparison with that required in the capture of a six-foot tarpon on a six-ounce rod and six-strand line? A six-foot tarpon will weigh about one hundred and twenty pounds, and the line will bear a deadweight strain of twelve pounds. Compare this with the three-pound trout taken on a gut leader, the weakest link in the angler's chain, which will lift a weight of two or more pounds, and the futility of beguiling oneself with the belief that the trout has any advantage will be apparent.

The playing of a trout is undeniably part of the sport, but, however difficult one wishes to make it, is but secondary to the pleasure derived from casting the fly and deluding that old trout into mistaking it for a bit of living food. It is this art, this skill, this study of the fish itself and its habits, that places dry fly fishing for trout far ahead of all other forms of angling. It has been said that there is no sport that requires in its pursuit a greater knowledge of the game, more skill, more perseverance, than fly fishing, and that no sport holds its votaries longer. I am quite of this opinion. "There is no genuine enjoyment in the easy achievement of any purpose," and in fly fishing a full measure of satisfaction is obtained only when the taking of a single fish is accomplished under conditions most difficult and trying.

The true angler is content only when he feels that he has taken his fish by the employment of unusual skill. The highest development of this skill at the present state of the angler's art is the dry fly method. I do not deny that there are many anglers who have carried sunk fly and even worm casting to a high degree of specialisation and refinement; yet it seems to me—nay, more than that, it is a positive conviction with me— that no manner of sunk fly or worm or bait casting bears any sort of favourable comparison to the manner of the dry fly. I know that in this country, at least, the dry fly man is accused by his sunk fly fellows of being affected, dogmatic, fanatic. Yet it is not so. The dry fly man has passed through all of the stages of the angler's life, from the cane pole and the drop-line to the split bamboo and the fur-and-feather counterfeit of the midge fly. He has experienced throes of delight each time he advanced from the lower to the higher grade of angler. I insist that I do not make my words too strong when I say that in all of angling there is no greater delight than that which comes to the dry fly angler who simulates a hatch of flies, and entices to the surface of the water a fish lying hidden, unseen, in the stronghold of his own selection. Let him who doubts put aside his prejudice long enough to give the premier method fair trial, and soon he will be found applying for the highest degree of the cult—"dry fly man."

CHAPTER VIII
A FEW PATTERNS OF FLIES

The literature devoted to the subject of the artificial fly is very extensive and informing, and it is not my intention to add thereto except for the purpose of describing a few flies that I use in my own fishing. The tackle shops offer almost countless patterns of flies of varied hues and forms, and anglers can indulge their individual tastes by choosing sizes, colours, and shapes to suit their fancies. I have never attempted to compute the number of artificial flies listed in the dealers' catalogues and described in the works of angling writers, but I think it must run into the hundreds. There is, however, a growing tendency toward restriction in the number of special patterns used in actual fishing, and in my own fishing I have reduced this number to a very small one.

It is doubtless true that the fly fisher derives no small part of his pleasure from the act of selecting and purchasing flies. It is within the experience of every fly fisher, I think, that, under the influence of the memory of a certain fish taken on a particular pattern of fly, he includes a dozen or two of the sort in his next purchase. Perhaps the fly is a nondescript that he may never again find successful, but, nevertheless, he adds it to his store. Angling friends recommend their patterns to him, or some special flies they found taking under certain circumstances or over particular streams, and these, too, he buys and puts away. Maybe he may never use one of them, and in the end he comes, perhaps, to feel, as does the philatelist, great pleasure in the possession of a worthy collection: he has the pride of ownership, but no thought of putting his treasures to use. Of course, there can be no reasonable objection to fly collecting, and I can see how it may become as fascinating an employment as stamp or coin collecting.

Assuming that the angler is a believer in close imitation, he will, of course, be content only when he has all the patterns which have been created by the votaries of the theory; but if he should be inclined to agree with me—that a great part of the imitation must be produced by the angler himself while actually fishing the stream— he will find that about ten patterns will suffice under nearly all circumstances.

I give the dressings of eight patterns, although I rarely use over six. If I were compelled to do so, I could get along very well with one—the Whirling Dun. Fishing the Brodhead throughout the month of July, I used this fly exclusively, and took fish every day except two. On three separate occasions I used a different fly—at one time a Pink Lady, at another a Mole, and at still another a Silver Sedge. On each occasion I took one fish with the selected fly, after which I went back to the Whirling Dun, and continued my fishing. I killed one or two fish each day, the average for the month being very close to a pound and a half. I returned many fish to the water, and these averaged over ten inches. Some days the fish were feeding, and some days they were not. There was apparently little difference in the taking effect of the fly, except that it was taken readily when it was delivered properly, and never when it was not.

No matter how great the faith an angler has in a single pattern, it will naturally be very difficult for him to confine himself to its exclusive use. So much of his sport depends

FLIES FROM LA BRANCHE, PATTERNS, PAGES 153-155

FLIES TIED BY DAVID LEDLIE AND PHOTOGRAPHED BY DOUG O'LOONEY

Whirling Dun

Pale Evening Dun

Pink Lady

Gold-Ribbed Hare's Ear

Flight's Fancy

Silver Sedge

Willow

Mole

"I could get along very well with one [fly pattern]—the Whirling Dun."

upon its delightful uncertainty, that if he does confine himself to the use of the single pattern, he will, of a consequence, be denied the pleasure of congratulating himself upon the acumen he has shown by the selection of the fly which is taken, after the favourite has been refused.

With the exception of the Pink Lady, the flies described are all standard patterns—tied, however, according to my own preference. Anglers who wish a more varied choice, one that includes one or two fancies, may add to the list a Wickham's Fancy and, for use when the fish are smutting, a small black gnat tied with a glossy black hackle and no wings—a variety that will often prove very effective when the fish are feeding in that manner. A Marlow Buzz may be included for use on windy days when the larger land insects are blown upon the water.

The flies commonly used by me, with their dressings, are as follows:

WHIRLING DUN (BLUE)
Wings. —Starling or duck, medium light.
Body. —Water-rat or mole fur; two turns of flat gold tinsel around hook at end of body.
Legs. —Glossy ginger or light brown cock's hackle.
Tail. —Three whisks of same.

PALE EVENING DUN (WATERY DUN)

Wings. —Light starling.
Body. —Lemon mohair lightly dressed.
Legs —Glossy barred Plymouth Rock cock's hackle.
Tail. —Two or three whisks of same.

PINK LADY

Wings. —Medium starling or duck.
Body. —Pale pink floss ribbed with flat gold tinsel.
Legs. —Ginger or light reddish-brown hackle.
Tails. —Three whisks of same.

GOLD-RIBBED HARE'S EAR

Wings. —Medium starling or duck.
Body. —Hare's fur ribbed with flat gold tinsel body, not too heavy.
Legs. —Hare's fur tied on with silk.
Tail. —Two or three rather long whisks, grey mallard.

FLIGHT'S FANCY

Wings. —Light starling or duck.
Body. —Pale yellow floss ribbed with flat gold tinsel.
Legs. —Ginger hackle.
Tail. —Two or three whisks of same.

The body of this fly will turn green when wet, which is nothing against it, however.

SILVER SEDGE

Wings. —Rather dark starling.
Body. —White floss ribbed with flat silver tinsel.
Legs. —Pale ginger hackle.
Tail. —Two or three whisks of same.

The body of this fly will turn a greyish-blue when wet, but the change does not affect its taking qualities.

WILLOW

Wings. —None.

Body. —Light blue fur, mole or fox, ribbed with light yellow silk.

Legs. —Glossy white or transparent hackle.

Tail. —Two whisks of same.

MOLE

Wings. —Medium starling or duck.

Body. —Light mole fur lightly dressed and tightly wound.

Legs. —Purplish-brown (dyed), hackle tied palmer-wise.

Tail. —Three or four whisks of same.

The standard pattern of this fly is tied with light brown woodcock wings.

It is advisable that each of the patterns be tied on hooks of different sizes—Nos. 10, 12, 14, and 16 will suffice—because the size of the fly is often important, particularly when the water is very low and clear.

If a greater aid is required in floating the fly (barring the use of paraffin) other than a stiff hackle at the shoulder, I would recommend that a short-fibred hackle be tied on at the shoulder and carried around and down the body to the tail, the fibres being cut off close to the body after tying. The effect of this dressing will be to make the fly float better, particularly after some use, and after the points of the longer shoulder hackles have been submerged. The short fibres along the body, by intercepting some light and permitting some to pass through, will help to produce the effect of transparency or translucency of the natural insect, which effect would be particularly noticeable upon flies where quill is used for the body. The use of this hackle can be dispensed with in the case of those flies where fur or mohair is used for the body—a few fibres picked out with a needle producing much the same appearance and effect.

It may be the experience of other anglers who have experimented with the artificial fly in attempts to produce one that would cock readily and maintain a good balance on the water, that one tied with the wings leaning rather more forward than is the present practice, offers the nearest solution to these difficulties. My own experience is that flies tied in this manner sit beautifully upon the water, but I cannot say that they cock any more frequently than those tied with upright wings. I would suggest that the angler tie a few flies with the wings tilted forward at an angle of about 120°, and try them. If nothing else is accomplished, the experiment may lead to a development in the form of the fly which will enable us all to some day take the one "big fish."

"My own experience is that flies tied in this manner [with the wings tilted forward at an angle of about 120 degrees] sit beautifully upon the water."

APPENDIX 1
CASTING THE CURVE

When La Branche published *The Salmon and the Dry Fly* in 1924, he built upon the theories of presentation that he introduced in *The Dry Fly and Fast Water*. As he pointed out, much of the material in *The Salmon and the Dry Fly* applied to trout as well as salmon.

Most importantly, La Branche introduced his description of what he dubbed the "curved cast." La Branche described the purpose of the curved cast on salmon rivers to be:

(1) To avoid drag

(2) To keep as much of the leader as possible away from the fish.

This rationale applies equally well to trout streams. La Branche spent the better part of the chapter describing the curved cast and its variations. Throughout the chapter he repeatedly apologized for his alleged inability to explain the cast. The apology is gratuitous; his explanation, peppered with tidbits of river-borne wisdom about how to solve difficult casting problems, reveals the myriad virtues of the curved cast, and La Branche's keen understanding of the mechanics of the cast.

La Branche notes that there are actually two curved casts—a right-hand curved cast (labeled cast number 1 in the illustration) and a left-hand curved cast (labeled cast number 2 in the illustration), as viewed from the perspective of a right-handed caster. (The left-handers among us will simply have to transpose La Branche's explanation to the left hand.) In LaBranche's frame of reference, the left-hand curved cast is achieved by overpowering the cast, and the right-hand cast by under

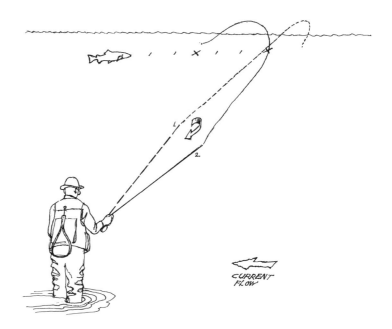

*The right-handed curve cast (#1) requires the angler to under-
power the forward cast. The left-handed curve cast (#2) requires
the angler to overpower the forward cast. Note the 45- degree
angle of the rod on the left-handed curve cast.*

powering. Being right-handed, La Branche always used
the left-handed cast to the left-hand bank, and the right-
handed cast to the right-hand bank, as he looked
upstream.

LaBranche addresses the left-hand cast first, offering
the following advice:

      1) cast three or more feet upstream of the fish;

      2) make sure the length of the cast extends
      beyond the fish about three feet; and

      3) just as the line straightens, pull back the the
      rod tip just enough to stop the fly in its forward
      flight.

By stopping the fly in its flight (La Branche called this "checking") it "will be thrown downstream . . . . A sharp curve will be the result, and what has seemed impossible will prove to be very simple." He places great emphasis on holding the rod at least at a 45-degree angle. He points out that the closer to the horizontal plane the rod is held, the sharper the curve that will be formed with the cast.

In describing the right-handed curved cast, LaBranche, ever heretical, asserts that the angler must "lose control of the line." He then goes on to concisely describe the deliberate loss of control:

> 1) Measure the distance by false casting, and as with the left-hand cast, extend enough line to overshoot the target;
> 2) When the desired distance is reached, "imagine that the casting line has neither fly nor leader attached to it," and before the final forward cast has fully extended, prematurely release the line held in the line hand, so that the energy of the cast "is diverted to pulling out the loose line" instead of extending the cast.

When done properly, the end of the line should land on target, and the fly should land to the right of it, with the leader forming a curve between the end of the line and the fly. La Branche makes the point that it is not necessary with the right-handed curve cast to hold the rod at a 45-degree angle.

LaBranche then makes the point—all too often missed by the modern angler, and incessantly preached by guides everywhere—that line control after the cast is essential. He urges the angler to follow the fly as it floats downsteam with the rod and to strip in any excess slack during the float. His prescription is as valid today as it was in 1924.

In describing the curved cast, La Branche offered a tool as valuable for trout fishing as for pursuing salmon and as useful on fast water as on slow water.

APPENDIX 2
SELECTIONS FROM THE SKUES–LA BRANCHE
CORRESPONDENCE, 1925-1947

George Edward Mackenzie Skues (1858-1949) is one of the central figures of twentieth-century fly-fishing theory. The foremost British proponent of nymph fishing, he had an enormous influence on fly fishermen in Europe and North America. His rivalry and literary debate with Frederic Halford, the leading British dry-fly writer, has been described by countless later writers. In the relatively open and unstructured world of modern fly fishing, it seems almost amazing that the choice of fly type—dry or wet—could generate the sort of hostility and bitterness it did early in this century, when Skues, Halford, and their various supporters squared off year after year in the sporting press, but that's how it was. It might make us wonder how many of our carefully nurtured opinions will someday be judged equally silly.

To the extent that anyone could win such a debate, Skues did, though it must not have seemed that way to him at the time of his death. As these letters show, disapproval of his methods by his fellow fishermen forced him off the Itchen in 1938, after he had fished that water for fifty-six seasons. But though today most of us still prefer one type of fishing or another (and may even look down on people who disagree with us), we are less inclined to the degree of blind bigotry that would compel us to actually exclude people with other tastes from the water.

Skues left a powerful theoretical and literary legacy in his hundreds of articles and letters, but most readers know him from his books: *Minor Tactics of the Chalkstream* (1910), *The Way of a Trout with a Fly*

(1921), *Sidelines, Sidelights, and Reflections* (1932), *Nymph Fishing for Chalkstream Trout* (1939), and several collections of his works published after his death, including *Silk, Fur and Feather* (1950), *Itchen Memories* (1951), *Angling Letters of G.E.M. Skues* (1956), and *G.E.M. Skues, The Way of a Man with a Trout* (1977).

When I first began reading about fishing, I had trouble finding the usefulness in Skues' work; his fishing, on carefully manipulated, privately managed chalkstreams seemed to have nothing to do with my fishing on the freestone streams of the American mountains. Over time, however, I recognized subtler wisdoms in his work, and from the beginning I was taken with the charm and easy humor of his stories. He is that rarest of fishing experts, the kind who can be an engaging writer at the same time that he is a good teacher.

Those two qualities also describe George La Branche, of course. La Branche is to the American dry fly what Skues is to the British nymph. Neither really originated their sport, but both pioneered, by codifying and refining older ideas and practices. It is an entertaining irony that these two men, so closely identified with opposite styles of fly fishing—La Branche with the freestone dry fly, Skues with the chalkstream nymph—should have hit it off so well and maintained such a long and warm correspondence. But of course, outside of the stereotyping given them by simplistic angling histories, they were both very open-minded fishermen, with an intense curiosity about the whole game.

The La Branche angling papers at Princeton are something of a miscellany: portions of published manuscripts, the occasional letter to this or that fishing writer, a few fragmentary journals. The most extended, and therefore interesting, portion of the collection is La

Branche's correspondence with Skues. What follows is an attempt at "high-grading" that material for items of most interest to modern fishermen and students of fishing writing. Their letters, like most of our letters, covered many subjects besides fishing, including world affairs, the doings of friends, personal life, and the weather. Except where one of them said something really curious or revealing on some other subject (such as La Branche's singular Depression-era observation that only a monarchy or dictatorship could save America from ruin), I have excerpted only from those letters that dealt with fishing. Even in the fishing material, I have been a bit selective, leaving out a number of long, dry passages dealing with the details and tribulations of leasing this or that water for fishing.

I recognize that this sort of selection is the result of a fundamentally subjective process; someone else might have found other parts of the correspondence more interesting than I did. But I assume that most readers of this book are not anxious to wade through too much extraneous matter to get to the fun stuff. What is left after this winnowing process is certainly fun for me, and may be for others. Those familiar with this century's fishing literature will find a number of eyebrow-raisers, for example both men's candid observations on the books of Edward Ringwood Hewitt, self-proclaimed pioneer of American nymph fishing.

But most of all you will find a comfortable conversation, the sort that more fishing books need. La Branche and Skues, as they appear here, are much like the rest of us in some respects. Fishing sometimes seems a blessing in an otherwise complicated world, a fresh and welcome stimulation of the mind and body, and an opportunity to share something good and untroubled with others. Around that sharing, as years and then decades pass, enduring friendships flourish, memories accumulate, and what matters about the fishing life is somehow revealed.

Light commentary, to introduce some of the characters mentioned by the correspondents, for example, has been added between some of the letters. If you need more detail, I can recommend you read Skues' books, any or all of them.

Paul Schullery

Note to the reader: La Branche's letters reproduced here are from his file copies and therefore are not signed. Skues' letters are the signed originals received by La Branche. Their styles of citing titles vary; for convenience all titles are italicized or in quotation marks, as appropriate. Unless otherwise noted, all of Skues' letters are from London. La Branche's file copies have no return addresses, but were probably written from New York (unless otherwise noted). Minor typographical errors have been corrected. Ellipses indicate omitted sections, and brackets indicate material that is illegible.

These letters are reproduced from the George M. L. La Branche Papers and published with permission of Princeton University Library.

June 4, 1925
Dear Mr. Skues:

A hurried decision is bringing me to England. I am leaving on June 17th and will be in London before you could reply to this note. It would give me great pleasure to know that I might have the privilege of calling upon you upon my arrival.

It is my present intention to secure a motor car for perhaps two or three weeks and travel about looking at your streams and learning your ways on them. My son, who is fourteen, will be my only companion, and he is quite keen on fly fishing. If you will advise me regarding some of the open waters in England and perhaps one or two trout streams in Scotland, I shall try to show my appreciation. I am keenly anxious to have my boy fish a few of your best streams (not club waters), so that in later years when he becomes the expert fly fisherman I expect he will, he will have a recollection of having been with his father on a jaunt through the greatest sporting country in the world.

By this mail I am sending you a copy of my book *The Salmon and the Dry Fly*. You may not like it any more than I do, but at least you can find little fault with its beautiful cover.

Please do not answer this letter to New York. If you feel inclined to reply at all, my address will be care of Morgan, Harjes & Company, London, but I shall make it my business to call you on the telephone shortly after my arrival.

Yours faithfully,

In the decade after 1912, La Branche, Edward Ringwood Hewitt, and Ambrose Monell devoted considerable energy to developing flies and methods for taking Atlantic salmon on the dry fly. This work resulted in La Branche's other book, *The Salmon and the Dry Fly* (1924), and was chronicled in Hewitt's writings as well, including *Secrets of the Salmon* (1922) and *A Trout and Salmon Fisherman for Seventy-Five Years* (1948). As in so many of the developments in fly fishing, there is some jockeying for position among the supposed originators of a new theory or technique. We see a little of this in the following letter, responding to an apparent concern on La Branche's part over the way the *British Fishing Gazette* treated his contributions.

Notice also Skues' mention of the "F.F.C." This is the famed Fly Fisher's Club of London.

September 8, 1925
My dear La Branche,

. . .

I am sincerely sorry to hear you have been having [d——] of Pneumonia. I think you are lucky to escape. I had it in both lungs in 1892, and if it had not been for a voyage which I took to the Cape in April to June 1893, I should probably have been measured for a wooden suit before very long. I went out weighing 10-stone 5-lbs. and came back weighing 12-stone 12-lbs., and though I was rather soft for two years, I have had practically nothing to spend on Doctors on my own account since, with the exception that I sprained an ankle rather badly. I never expected to reach 40, but I am now 67, and am taking an intolerable long time adying, like King Charles II.

I am surprised to see that you say that you dislike using a single handed rod on a salmon river. According to the accounts which I have been reading in the *Fishing Gazette* you were fishing a 12-footer and a 14-footer single-handed, which struck me as rather a feat for a slight man.

I am trying to get several of my friends to copy your methods on comparatively smooth flowing salmon rivers.

. . .

I think you have got the wrong end of the stick about the remarks in the *Fishing Gazette* on the subject of you and Hewitt being the pioneers in the fishing of the dry fly for salmon. A member of the Fly Fishers' Club, Mr. C.A.N. Wauton, wrote a notice in the *Fishing Gazette* on your colleague's Film Show, and in that he described you and Hewitt as the first to practise fishing the salmon with the dry fly, and I think that nothing more was meant by the comments than that you had had a predecessor on this side in Major Fraser, now deceased; but I assure you there is no disposition whatever to deprive you and Hewitt of the credit to which you are undoubtedly entitled of being the first to raise the method to a practical system. Fraser's flies may be seen illustrated in Farlow's catalogue somewhere about 1903, but they never took anything of a hold, and he never wrote a book on the subject. I, myself, have had heaps of credit for putting into simple English practices which must have been not infrequently more or less unconsciously adopted by many predecessors, so you must not be sensitive of what was not a criticism of you, but merely a rallying to the defence of another man.

I note that you are thinking of coming over in April of next year. I must remember to keep you a week end in May for the Itchen. Birch usually has the first week end of the fishing, which is the last week end in April, because he is up in Town for the purpose of the Academy Exhibition, to which he usually sends some pictures.

Your friend Lord appears to have been so pleased with his reception over here that he wrote to a partner of his named Bradley, whom you may know, advising him to look us up. I invited him, Bradley, to dinner at the F.F.C. And found him an extremely pleasant fellow, and Fraser asked him down to fish the Kennett for a day this week, and offered to lend him rods and tackle, but whether Bradley will be able to do it or not, I am not sure, but I think he means to try.

Yours very truly,
G.E.M. Skues

In the next letter, La Branche mentions salmon fishing with "Wood." This was A. H. E. Wood, whose pioneering work in "greased-line fishing" resulted in Jock Scott's book *Greased Line Fishing for Salmon* (1935). Chapter nine in Scott's book is an extended discussion of dry-fly fishing for salmon on Wood's home water on the Dee, in Scotland, written in good part by La Branche. Interestingly, in that chapter, La Branche says that at the time of his 1925 visit and fishing, he had not fished at all for four years. He apparently returned to the Dee three or four times after 1925.

La Branche (left) with greased-line pioneer A. H. E. (Arthur) Wood
CHARLES PHAIR, *ATLANTIC SALMON FISHING* [1937]

January 15, 1926
Dear Skues:

I have just received your letter, delayed in some unaccountable manner, informing me that the Fly Fishers Club had extended me the privilege of the Club House again this coming season. Will you be good enough to convey to them my appreciation of this courtesy and say that I shall with great pleasure avail myself of the opportunity to visit their rooms.

If my plans are not disarranged I will leave here on April 21st., when I go after a day or two in London, immediately to Scotland to visit Wood and try the dry fly over salmon under conditions quite different from those with which I met in July last. If Wood does not expect me too soon after my arrival, I shall give myself the pleasure of calling upon you and asking you to dine with me some evening before I go. In any event, I shall return to London before the end of May, when I hope you will be able to spare a little time to talk fishing with me.

My reception in England upon my recent visit was so flattering that I am still warm with thoughts of it. I am impatient to get back to tell you all how grateful I am.

Unfortunately, my boy will be at school and I shall be denied an interesting companion. However, two of my daughters will be abroad about that time and I expect to meet them in London to accompany them home.

Always with best regards.
Yours faithfully,

May 5, 1926
My dear La Branche,

I have been kicking myself during the last few days for my omission to tell you that R. Atkin Fraser (The Mill House, Ramsbury-[?]-on the Kennett) asked me when he heard you were coming over to say that he would be very pleased to give you a day or two on his water on the Kennett. If you are by any chance hung up by this strike, you could no doubt motor down to Ramsbury and get a pleasant day or two. He said I might come too, but business will not permit this. It looks as if this strike would put my fishing in the pot for some time. I hope, however, not too long to prevent your visiting the Itchen during your visit. It is rotten luck that the strike should come while you are with us.

On Friday I met a friend just back from fishing with Wood on the Dee. He said he had 22 salmon in I think 10 days and Bostock (of the F.F.C.) had 50 in a rather longer time. He had tried the floating fly, but with no luck, and he feared you would find the river too high. I told another man who knows the river of the successes of these two men, and he said Cairnton was a cannery—or if it was'nt it ought to be.

Wishing you tight lines,
Yours ever,
G.E.M. Skues

Edward Ringwood Hewitt, at times a friend and at times a rival of La Branche's, published *Telling on the Trout* in 1926. Judging from the comments of Skues and La Branche in the next two letters, it was not well received in all circles.

July 1, 1926
Dear Skues:

. . .

I remember that you asked me when I was in London whether or not Hewitt was preparing a book on trout fishing for publication and I told you then that I was not aware of it. I was rather surprised to learn at the Fly Fishers Club the last night we were there, that he had written one and even more surprised when I read it here that he wrote it at all. There is really no reason for its having come into being as far as I can see. If you will not consider it in the nature of a gift, I shall forward to you shortly a copy for your library.

A letter came to me yesterday from Bostock in which he said he was quite relieved to know that I had been unable to get to the Itchen, as the fishing had been so poor and the weather almost impossible.

Always my best regards.
Yours faithfully,

July 12, 1926
My dear La Branche,

I am sincerely sorry to hear that you have had Bronchitis and that your boy has had to have his tonsils out. I can never understand why it is considered legitimate to cut out an organ with which the Almighty has probably endowed man because it is of some service to him. However, the Doctors know better.

You appear to have shared bad weather with us. Nearly every week-end that I have been down at Winchester this season until the last week-end the wind has been dead down stream, and it made the fishing extremely difficult. This week-end turned suddenly so hot that the fishing was practically no easier, at any rate for the big fish. The week-end before last I got a trout of 2-lb 15 oz. and yesterday I lost one which must have been 24ins long, and when I tried to get my net under him, although it was 18ins across, he lapped over both sides, and just as I was getting him up to the net a second time, he came unstuck.

I am glad to hear that you will make a point of visiting the Itchen next year. Lamorna Birch's address is Lamorna, Near Penzance. I have written to him as you suggest.

It is very good of you to offer Hewitt's book to the F.F.C. but I think they have already two copies, and he was kind enough to send me one with some sort of personal dedication in it. I am amused to see your comments upon it—almost as amused as I was at some of Hewitt's spelling such as 'Teste' and 'Ichin'.

With kind regards,
Yours sincerely,
G.E.M. Skues

July 23, 1926
My dear La Branche,

I have this morning received your kind gift of Hewitt's new book. You will have heard from me by now that he had himself presented me with a copy, but in view of the more than kind personal dedication which you have written in the fly leaf, I shall have much pleasure in installing both copies in my Angling library.

Hewitt paid me a call a day or two ago with his elongated son, and I had arranged to dine at the Fly Fishers' Club last night to meet him and see his Kinema show of some kind of fishing or another, but for certain reasons which I need not go into, I found myself unable at the last moment to be present. I was sorry because I should very much like to have seen them. His previous show was most interesting. I believe he is off to Germany next week. He told me he wanted to make me the subject of one of his films, though how he is going to indicate on a film that I was fishing a Nymph tied on a 00. or 000. hook I do not know. His idea was to catch me bending on the Itchen. He would say Ichin.

I am sorry that your friend Bradley has not been over this year as we took a great fancy to him over here.

With kind regards and again many thanks,
Cordially yours,
G.E.M. Skues

November 17, 1926
My dear La Branche,

I was looking over the Fishing Tackle Catalogue of Alexr. Martin of 20 Exchange Square, Glasgow, when I came across an item which I thought might interest you if you do not already know about it. It is headed "The Dry Fly for Salmon" and is called the "H.W." (meaning Harold Wilson) Series. There are two illustrations, each of a body with stiff cocks hackle at head and tail and one has hackle point wings. The patterns of which there are four (or eight if you treat the hackle point wings as constituting an additional pattern) are based on an idea which has for many years been in use over here for especially large mayflies and was the invention of a lately deceased Angler named Horace Brown and by him named the Fore and Aft. I never used them as, though they undoubedly took trout when they had gone daft on Mayfly they destroyed any likeness to the natural fly. Horace Brown was for many years President of the Piscatorial Society and one of the most charming old fellows I ever met. Witty, but without a particle of malice in him. I never heard him say an unkind thing about a soul. The Kennet at Newbury and Hungerford was his pet beat. I tried several times to induce him to join the F.F.C. but never succeeded.

Would you like to have a copy of Martin's Catalogue?

With kind regards,
Yours sincerely,
G.E.M. Skues

December 18, 1926
Dear Skues:

Thank you so much for the Alexander Martin catalogue. I was particularly interested in the so-called "Fore and After" flies which are depicted, because this is exactly the type of fly with which I took my fish on the Test at Stockbridge.

I had some flies tied up in this manner with the idea that they would float higher from the surface of the water than the ordinary dry fly, having the fly float on the points of its hackles is one of my delusions. It has almost become an obsession. There is really nothing new under the sun, but I have been using this pattern for a number of years now, and probably couldn't throw any other decently. I have not applied the principle to salmon fishing particularly, because the flies used over these fish are so much larger that they rest quite well on the water because of their longer hackles.

I am off for a week's duck shooting with my small son Bob, and will drop you a line upon my return.

My boy joins me in sending you best wishes for the Holiday season, and we both hope that the New Year will be full of all good things for you.

Yours faithfully,
P.S. You will probably hear from Lord with regard to the leasing of the cottage on the Kennet to Mr. St. George. If Mr. St. George gets in touch with you and you have a copy of the lease, it might be well to call his attention to that part of it which limits the fishing to three days per week to any tenant leasing from us.

The "Major Hills" mentioned by Skues in the next letter is John Waller Hills, author of *A History of Fly Fishing for Trout* (1921), *A Summer on the Test* (1924), and *Riverkeeper: The Life of William James Lunn* (1934). Skues uses a string of periods to indicate passage of time.

January 4, 1927
Dear La Branche,

If you have, or can get hold of, a copy of F.M. Halford's *An Angler's Autobiography* you can see at p. 201 a very good picture of Ramsbury Mill House where Fraser lives, and at p. 206 a picture of Moon's Mill—about half way up the fishing from the Mill House and therefore a bit below the Cottage. The Chapter beginning p. 197 "The Kennett & Making a Fishery" tells what F.M.H. did for or rather to the Water. I have often thought that all that tidying up was unsound in principle. Contrast the wonderful Mayfly sport of their first season with the disappointments of the ensuing three. Nature has a way of knowing best and though wildness may be overdone, so too may grooming.

. . . .

The above had been written when your letter of the 18th December reached me (on the 3rd January)—I wonder why so long on the way?

I think there can be no doubt that, whatever others may have done in the same directon—old Horace Brown's Fore & Aft flies (Mayflies I believe in the first instance) were his own invention, independent of any other. It may be my delusion but, whatever may be done on the Test, I doubt whether my Itchen trout would be lured by Fore & Afters. But I hope you will have an opportunity of trying one day in the coming season.

Apropos of the Test, old Coggeshall's daughter Mrs. Home presented to me in November her Father's copy of the *Chronicles* of the Houghton Club presented to him by Arthur N. Gilbey the Secretary, and I wrote to tell Gilbey of it and mentioned your visit. He told me that you were <u>his</u> guest. I thought you had been Major Hill's.

It is hoped that our Prime Minister Baldwin will be the Guest of Honour at the Annual Dinner of the F.F.C. on the 24th January. He has been attacked by Lloyd George and some other 'lewd fellows of the baser sort' for his settlement of the British debt to your Country. I have always admired him for acting without hesitation or qualification on the principle that this Country must honour its bond. There are to be no other guests I believe because the Hall of the Fishmongers' Company where the Dinner is to be held is only capable of seating 150, and I doubt whether all the members wanting seats will get them.

Many thanks to you and your boy for your good wishes. I cordially, if somewhat tardily, reciprocate them. I think he is a lucky lad to have a father who is not only willing, but able to put him in the way to be a great sportsman while he is young enough to learn. Nothing will ever compensate one for missing, as I did, the experience of fly fishing practice from the age of 11 or so on. It is most exceptional for any one who begins to learn in or after the twenties to become really first rate.

With K.R. to you both and hoping to see you soon,
Yours ever,
G.E.M. Skues

January 28, 1927
Dear Skues:

Thank you so much for arranging to have the Fly Fishers Club Journal sent to me. I have already received a copy of the last issue, and shall send Mr. Kent a draft for the cost, although I do not know what the additional postage is for the United States.

I quite agree with you that tidying up a stream quite frequently is very harmful. It is unwise to meddle with nature in any way. Certainly, we cannot improve upon it.

I thought you knew that I was Gilbey's guest at the Houghton Club, and that Hewitt had been invited by Major Hill. For my part, I would have been glad to go down as guest of either or both of these gentlemen, and I am still of that mind.

How I wish I could be with you for the annual dinner. I have just had to make a speech myself at the annual dinner of the Anglers Club here, a thing that I loathe, and I imagine my audience is never very keen about hearing me.

You will perhaps have heard from Lord by now, with regard to the subleasing of the cottage to Mr. St. George. I am sorry that this has been messed up, as it was never my intention to give it up. The only reason I considered it at all, was because the furniture which I had hoped to buy, had been removed. The last letter that Lord showed me, which was either from you or Mr. St. George, indicated that he wished to take over the cottage and the fishing, and limited us to the fishing rights for one month. This is utterly ridiculous from my standpoint, and I would not think of abrogating my right to fish for the entire length of my stay in England, even to be nice to Mr. St. George or anybody else. If Mr. St. George wants the cottage as a home, and can take advantage of the clause in the lease which permits him to fish three days a week, when neither Lord nor myself are there, I would be inclined to let him have it. I intend to spend three months in England, and must feel at liberty to go to the stream whenever I wish, and stay as long as I please. I hope to entertain some American sportsmen as well as my British friends, and I am not inclined to enter any engagement with Mr. St. George which will prevent me from doing so. I am sorry if there has been a misunderstanding, but certainly nothing was ever said that either Lord's fishing, or my own, should be limited to one month. Mr. St. George assumed that we would hurry back for our Canadian fishing. Where he got this idea, I have no way of knowing, because I had no intention of going to Canada.

I am sorry that you have been put to so much trouble, and I am quite willing to make some concession, but not to the extent of practically abandoning my privilege to visit the stream when I please without asking somebody's permission. Mr. St. George must have known that I intended to spend some time in Great Britain, because when I saw his son here, I told him so, and told him also that I would be glad to have his father as my guest when nobody else was there.

My best regards always,
Yours faithfully,

February 7, 1927
Dear La Branche,

My little Club on the Itchen has now settled its apportionment of guest weeks. Mine are as follows:

May 13th to 19th inclusive
June 3rd to 9th   "
June 24th to 30th   "
July 15th to 21st   "
August 5th to 11th   "

I imagine June 3rd to the 9th will correspond with your May Fly fishing on the Kennett, and that therefore you won't care to have that date, and June 24th, 25th and 26th are already allotted to my old friend McCaskie, who has a week-end with me whoever else goes without. But if you could manage to take a couple of days (I may only give two days in one week to any one guest) and take them during the week, I would make a point of being down with you, either in May, June, July or August. It would suit me better if you would come down during the week—that is to say for two days out of Monday, Tuesday, Wednesday and Thursday, because that would leave me free to have other friends on the week-ends when they can get away.

Yours sincerely,
G.E.M. Skues

March 7, 1927
Dear Skues:

I am sorry that I have not been able to find time to write you before, but I have been swamped during the past month. My partners have both been away and the market has been extremely active.

Thank you so much for your invitation to the Itchen. Of course I will be glad to fit in at any time that will suit your convenience. I can understand readily why men who are engaged in business affairs can only steal away at weekends. My time will be my own, and I hope there will be nothing to bother me, so that I can go in the first part or the middle of the week, as you please. Would it be asking too much of you to wait until I arrive early in May before I specify when I can go? I would like to conform to your own desires and fit in at a time when you feel that you are at liberty to go down.

I am leaving Thursday for some bonefishing in Florida and you may not hear from me again until just before I sail, so please don't feel that I am neglecting you.

Lord and I are looking forward to having you down on the Kennet. I am particularly anxious to have you come to have you point out to me, if you will, the improvement (?) made in the fishery there by Halford.

Always my best regards.
Yours faithfully,

September 21, 1927
My dear La Branche,

I have been expecting to hear from you as to what I am to do with your two copies of Vavon's book. I do not know whether you care about Angling Verse or whether you have read any of Patrick Chalmers' stuff. In my opinon there has been no-one who has written

Angling Verse to touch him since John Denny's centuries ago.

K.R. Yours sincerely,
G.E.M. Skues

In the next letter, Skues refers to Henry Andrews Ingraham's book *American Trout Streams* (1926), published in a very limited edition (150 copies) by what would soon become Derrydale Press for the Angler's Club of New York.

October 27, 1927
My dear La Branche,
I have received from you this morning and acknowledge with cordial thanks, the copy of Mr. Ingraham's book on American Trout Streams, privately printed for the Anglers Club of New York, together with a dedication to myself, which I think suggests that you must have been in Ireland and have kissed the Blarney Stone. I am looking forward to reading the book with great pleasure, and to lending it to a few selected friends. I believe it has already been noticed in one or more of the angling papers in England, but I do not recall exactly which.

Meanwhile, may I be so unkind as to remind you that you have never told me what you want me to do with the two copies of Vavon's great work, which are lying packed up here in my room awaiting your instructions.

With kind regards,
Yours sincerely,
G.E.M. Skues

Marguerite Ives, who figures in the next few letters, apparently got crosswise of both La Branche and Skues before her little literary adventure with them was over, but there must have been no hard feelings, at least on her side. In 1929, she included a glowing biography of La Branche in her book *Seventeen Famous Outdoorsmen*, an account, that for all of its adulation, does provide us with some of our few fishing-related quotations from La Branche in the 1920s.

October 31, 1927
Miss Marguerite Ives
'Outdoor America'
536 Lake Shore Drive
Chicago, U.S.A.

Dear Madam,

I duly received your letter of the 13th inst. I have a warm regard for Mr. George La Branche, and I should like to do anything I can that would oblige him. Dr. Henry Van Dyke is also a friend for whom I have a strong affection, and I am fully in sympathy with the objects of your magazine. The difficulty I feel is that I hardly know what subject you would wish me to treat, and I have never visited the U.S.A. and am only familiar to a certain extent with its angling problems through the works of Dr. Van Dyke, La Branche, E.R. Hewitt and one or two others. I have put practically all that I have to say that has any novelty on the subject of fly fishing, in my two books and various articles which have appeared in the *Field* and elsewhere, but if you or Mr. La Branche would make a suggestion as to what you would like me to write about, I would be pleased to do my best.

Very faithfully yours,
G.E.M. Skues

November 4, 1927
Miss Marguerite Ives

Dear Madam,

I took home your letter of the 13th October, together with the two copies of your magazine. I think that the effort which the Isaac Walton League is making in America is on a magnificent scale, and I could wish that something as strenuous and well thought out could be set on foot in this country.

When I wrote you I had not any ideas as to what I could put into an article for you, but in looking over my library I came across Orvis & Cheney's book *Fishing with the Fly* and that gave me the idea for the Paper which I now enclose. I hope it is the sort of thing that you want, and that it will be of some service to you, but I should like you to show it to my friend Mr. George La Branche before it is published, as he may think that it requires revision or reconsideration in consequence of my ignorance of some American conditions which are relevant.

With regard to payment, I have never written on angling matters deliberately for payment, though as a matter of principle and in fairness to others, when I contribute to papers which pay for a contribution, I accept payment at whatever rate is given so as not to compete unfairly with others who write for their living.

Yours faithfully,
G.E.M. Skues

November 4, 1927
My dear La Branche,

I have received from a Miss Marguerite Ives, the Editor of *Outdoor America* an eloquently worded letter containing an appeal, apparently instigated by yourself, to contribute an article or story to that Journal and enclosing me the October and November numbers. At the time when I received and acknowledged her letter I had no notion of a subject for such an article—but I have since evolved something which I hope may prove suitable, and in sending it to her I am asking her, before deciding to print it, to submit it to you. The object of this I have not told her, but it is this. I am anxious that nothing of mine should give offence on your side, and I am not sure that I have been entirely successful in avoiding points on which your compatriots or some of them might prove touchy. So if when you see the M.S. you think that there is anything in it which might offend, I shall be grateful if you will not let any supposed consideration for my feelings prevent you from saying so and from suppressing the contribution.

I have been reading the book on American Trout Streams which you sent me. It is written with much eloquence and charm as well as with sound sense—but I wish I had had the privilege of correcting the proofs, for honestly I cannot congratulate the proof reader on his work. Such words as Carniverous occur twice in one paragraph. On p. 77 Hymonoptera has been passed for Hymenoptera. 'Flies' in one place is spelt 'flys' and so on.

I am amazed at the account of Mayflies in such numbers as to break the boughs of willow trees and to clog the machinery of river steamers. I have seen hatches on our home waters which were heavy enough to make the water look foul with dead and dying flies, and the shucks of hatching flies, but that would not have been enough by 9990 per cent to break boughs and clog machinery. Yet it was enough to gorge all the trout to repletion and render them uncatchable. What then would be the effect of such a hatch as that described in your friend's book.

I see that he complains of the growing shortage of fly in some of your rivers—but if you have huge hatches normally, I should be inclined to wonder at your ever getting any trout with representations of the natural fly and to see in these huge hatches the justification and reason for the use of the garish flies depicted by Mrs.

Marbury and by Orvis & Cheney.

I am still looking forward to being made acquainted with your wishes as to the disposal of your two copies of Vavon's book. You will have to have them bound, for they will hardly hold together (as lightly stitched in their paper covers) through two readings. I am paying 26/- to have my own copy bound but the F.F.C. copy is costing £2.12.6. to bind. . . .

St. George has made a lovely place of his garden. He asked me down for a week-end in September, but little was doing with the trout for the weeds were foul with flannel weed coming down from Burdett's lake at the top of the water. I was broken three times in the first evening as the fish getting in among these clotted weeds could not be extricated.

I rather like that Payne rod of St. G's though it has more power than I want for general purposes.

I took McCaskie and a friend of his down to Winchester for a week-end with the Grayling in mid October and McCaskie had his boy out from the old School to share his rod and the friend used mine. In the Saturday afternoon and the following day the two rods killed about 25-lbs of Grayling in 24 fish. I am sorely afraid that they are going to be a nuisance again. Now I have put by my rods and tackle till 1928. It is almost six months before the next season begins, and as I am now in my 70th year I feel that more than I used to when I was younger.

With K.R.
Yours sincerely,
G.E.M. Skues

In this and several other letters, Skues refers to weed cutting. The streams he fished were much more intensively managed, in some ways, than most American trout streams. Cutting the sometimes overluxuriant growth of aquatic vegetation was an important duty of British riverkeepers. A good brief account of the rationale and techniques of weed cutting in a trout stream appears in Frank Sawyer's *Keeper of the Stream* (1952).

November 5, 1927
My dear La Branche,

Many thanks for your letter of the 28th inst. I am sorry to hear you have been laid up with Bronchitis, but I trust by the time this reaches you you will be quite all right again.

I acknowledged the book on Trout Streams the very day I received it, but that was not a long time ago as you say but only just over a week ago.

I shall be very pleased to keep Vavon's book for you till the Spring. I am not trying to get rid of it, but I was only anxious to know what you wanted about it, but perhaps you will make up your mind when you realise that it requires binding before it is really fit to use or present. I do not know whether Chalmers' Angling Verses are in print any longer, but I know that St. George bought copies of the two volumes *Green Days and Blue Days* and *A Peck o' Maut* both of which contain some delightful angling verse. I will look up the Publisher (somewhere in Dublin I think) and see if I can get you copies.

It is good to think you will be over again in the Spring, and I hope that we shall be able to hit upon a date when they are not cutting weeds, and when the weather is kinder than when you were with me this year. I do not know that I want the fish rising madly. I would rather they were rising sedately and not too often, because when they are rising madly there is usually too much fly, and every offer you make has to compete with a number of natural flies, and has very little chance. The difficulty about a date that does'nt clash with the weed cutting is that you want to be on your own water for the Mayfly, and therefore you must either come down in the earlier part of May when the weed-cutting is on or possibly just finished, or else you must leave it until your Mayfly fishing is over, and then I suppose you want to go up to the Dee.

With Kind regards,
Yours sincerely,
G.E.M. Skues

December 7, 1927
My dear La Branche,

I have just heard from Miss Ives, the Editor of *Outdoor America* saying that you have passed the Article I sent for that Journal so I infer that you think there is nothing to which your compatriots might take offence. She tells me it will appear in the January or February number.

I don't know whether you see the *Field*. If so, you may have seen that they printed a portrait of me in the number of the 17th November. The Angling Editor asked for a photograph to make a frontispiece to one of the series of Anglers, but when it came to the point the Chief Editor over-ruled the Angling Editor so it is only a reduced portrait that has been produced. It had been preceded a few weeks' earlier by a portrait of William Radcliffe, the author of *Fishing from Earliest Times* and he told me that a number of his friends had congratulated him and said what a good portrait it was, but that it made him say to himself "I had no idea what a d——d ugly old man I had become" and that is very much how I feel about my own, but most people seem to think it is a satisfactory performance.

You will probably be getting news shortly of the changes in connection with the F.F.C. They are putting up the subscription both of town and country members and are turning over the assets to a Company so as to have a Corporation which can enter into contracts and take leases without exposing the individual members or Trustees to personal liability. We shall be staying on for the next eight years in the present premises as efforts to find other premises have failed.

With kind regards,
Yours sincerely,
G.E.M. Skues

December 15, 1927
Dear Skues:

There is going forward to you shortly, if not already started on its way, a rod, with which I hope you will kill during the coming season, the largest trout in the Itchen.[1]

We have been so active in my business that I have had but few moments for my personal correspondence.

I have forgotten whether or not I asked you to keep Vavon's book for me until I come over in the Spring. If I did not, and it is not too much trouble to you, I should like very much to have you put it away.

Your interesting article in *The Field* with regard to the book, recalled to my mind the fact that you had mine in your possession. While the portrait of you on the same page is an excellent likeness, it is in no way flattering. When I come over in the Spring I shall help myself to one of them if you have any copies to spare, in exchange for which I shall be glad to give you one of myself.

Always my best wishes, and particularly at this season of the year.
Yours faithfully,

---

1. The rod La Branche refers to in this letter was one that he ordered as a gift for Skues from William Mills & Son of New York. According to the invoice, La Branche ordered "1 Leonard Tourn. Rod No. 51 D.F. - 9' - 5 oz. - Agate 1st Per. Tips". The rod cost $52.00 and was shipped directly to Skues.

American fishing book enthusiasts will recognize the name of Gene Connett in the next letter. The author of several fishing books, including *Any Luck?* (1933) and *My Friend the Trout* (1961), Connett was the founder of Derrydale Press, the distinguished little publishing firm that produced the first editions of many important sporting books of the 1930s and 1940s.

We also find out that the rod La Branche gave him was a Leonard. Skues had a particular weakness for some Leonard rods, and through much of his fishing career after 1905, Leonards were his favorites. One he received that year he often referred to as the "world's best rod."

December 28, 1927
My dear La Branche,

I was somewhat startled a day or two ago to receive from your friend Eugene V. Connett the announcement that, on his proposal, I had been elected to Honorary Membership of the Anglers Club of New York. Notwithstanding what he says I cannot help a feeling that you, with your ridiculous estimate of *Minor Tactics*, are somehow at the bottom of the business. If so, it is very kind of you, and I appreciate it. But I do not think there is a dog's chance of my ever being able to give myself a holiday in New York, so that the compliment of my election is likely to remain a compliment.

I heard from Miss Ives that you passed the article I sent for publication in *Outdoor America* from which I infer it did not strike you as likely to annoy your compatriots.

I am sending you a copy of the *Field* of 17th November which contains a portrait of me on page 796 with a small paragraph thereon, also the first part of my appreciation of Vavon's Book the second and final part being in the following weekly number.

From something I heard last autumn, I am forced to believe that Fraser, for some reason or lack of reason, has become unfriendly, and regards me as "a poacher"—so though I hope to see you on the Itchen in 1928 I do not think a return visit will be a possibility as I should hate to be fishing a man's water against his will. I believe St. George is away till April.

With kind regards, and all good wishes for 1928
Yours ever,
G.E.M. Skues
P.S. I have just received your letter of the 15th December. I had hoped that you had forgotten your threat to endow me with a new fly rod. I have already had one 9ft 6in from Mrs. Home (Coggeshall's daughter) this year as an acknowledgment of some services which, with the help of our mutual friend Lord, I did for her in connection

with her Mother's Estate.

Yes, I have two copies of Vavon's book for you. You asked me if it would be inconvenient to me to keep them for you until you came over, and I said 'No, I would keep them with pleasure' and they are available at a moment's notice.

I don't know whether there will be any copies of my portrait available when you come over in the Spring, but if not one is easily obtained as the Photographer is just over the way.

G.E.M.S.

On re-reading the above P.S. I see that I have very ungratiously failed to thank you as I should for your kindness in the matter of this fly rod. I am sure you know that I am not ungrateful but I have for so many years had to practice rigid economy in every direction that I feel that the bestowal on me of yet another Leonard, which I shall probably not live long enough to give the use it deserves, is a bit of a waste.

G.E.M.S.

January 2, 1928
My dear La Branche,

I have received from the Entertainment Committee of the Angling Club at New York, a notice of the Annual Dinner to be held on the 17th January, with Dr. Van Dyke as Toast Master. I suppose this is sent to me by virtue of the election announced to me by Mr. Connett. He, however, merely told me that he "saw" I had been elected, but I have received no official communication from the Secretary or other proper Officer of the Club. I shall be very interested to read the report of the Speeches in the Club Bulletin. Can one obtain that be subscribing to it? If so, I should like to do so. I must write to Van Dyke.

At the moment the Country is under a horrid mess of snow (rather deep for us) in a state of deliquescence. This I hope means that an enormous quantity of water will soak into the chalk and produce both for the Kennett and Itchen abundant supplies of water right through the season of 1928, for which I wish you tight lines.

Yours ever,
G.E.M. Skues

January 11, 1928
My dear La Branche,

The threatened rod has duly reached me this morning. Very many thanks indeed for it. It is most kind of you. I am very much relieved to find that it is not under 9-ft. It seems tremendously powerful for its length, and will certainly cast a Mayfly and would probably kill a fair sized Salmon without much difficulty if there were enough running line. I am looking forward to trying it and the 9ft 6in rod presented to me by Coggeshall's daughter, Mrs. Home, on my water before you are over in May, for I suppose that is when you will be coming.

A day or two ago I received the January number of *Outdoor America* with the article for which you let me in. I did'nt mind that so much, but what I did not count on was being let in for the paragraph, apparently quoted from you, with which the Editress has headed the article. I do wish she had'nt done it, as I asked her to send on copies to the F.F.C. and two or three friends over here; and I expect that they will be asking me "Did I get that 'boost' put in specially," and "what was the cost of the advertisement." My friends of the F.F.C. will be well aware how far that estimate has been deserved. *You* won't have to live it down, but I shall.

With kind regards and all good wishes for your 1928 season,
Yours ever,
G.E.M. Skues

January 16, 1928
My dear La Branche,

I received your letter of the 6th inst. and am glad to have the date of your coming over. I won't make you a suggestion yet as to when you should come down to me, because I should like to make sure when the weed-cutting is first, so as to avoid that. I had heard nothing from Lord as to when you propose to be over but on the strength of your letter I have written Mr. St. George asking him to take formal notice that you will be over on the 1st May and expect to be in the country for three months.

I put the new rod together yesterday, and tried it on the lawn, but I doubt whether the line that I put through the rings was quite heavy enough to develop its power, of which it possesses a good deal. In fact I think it will probably be equal to handling a small salmon without much strain. The terms in which you speak of it are very flattering, but what I feel about it is that I shan't live long enough to give it anything like the use that it deserves, and that in that sense it is rather thrown away upon me. I have already two 10-ft Leonards, one of them with two butts, two middles and 5 tops, two 9-footers one stiff and the other a bit more limber, and one 9-ft 6in, rather fine in the point, which reached me a little before yours, so I shall be hard put to it to know much to choose from time to time.

I am glad my Article in *Outdoor America* was approved of but for all that, I wish the Editress had'nt put that preliminary quotation from you in it.

With kindest regards,
Yours sincerely,
G.E.M. Skues

February 23, 1928
My dear Skues:

Dictating this letter to you from my bed where I am trying to recover from an operation which removed my tonsils last Saturday. I am told that I will be a great deal better after this and if I am not, I don't mind saying that I will have suffered a great deal in vain.

I was quite as much put out as you were that Miss Ives put in the paragraph that she did with your article. She asked me to tell her something about you so that she could write intelligently when she mentioned you editorially. I had no idea that she was to quote me verbatim, and before I received your letter I had written her remonstrating.

As soon as I am able to get on my feet I will be on my way to Florida for some bonefishing. Unless all my plans go askew, I will sail for England on the 18th of April, and I am looking forward with great anticipation to seeing you. . . .

Always my best regards.
Yours faithfully,

August 28, 1928
Dear Skues:

The Stock Market has had me by the ears for so long that I have not only not written my friends, but had almost forgotten that I had any.

Will write you a bit later to tell you of some wonderful salmon fishing that I had in July. The purpose of this letter is to prepare you for a visit of a friend of mine, Mr. William U. Goodbody, who is leaving shortly for England for a long stay. If you could give him a day on the Itchen either with you or alone, he would be profoundly impressed. He is a good angler and really a very fine sportsman, and a gentleman.

I am giving him a card to you.

Always my warmest regards.
Yours faithfully,

January 1, 1929

My dear La Branche,

This morning on arriving at my Office I found awaiting me not only your very kind cable of good will, but also your card with an illustration of alighting snipe, and by the same post I received a copy of the December number of the Anglers' Club Bulletin. Many thanks for your good wishes, which I cordially reciprocate. I tried to make out a likeness to yourself putting a fly across the Kennett, but you are a little difficult to recognise from the back view. I recognise the spot where you were fishing though. Was it Lord who was standing by you or who? I don't think it is old St. George.

I should like to tell you in confidence that a friend of mine has in the stocks a book which I think will prove to be when published a realisation of a hope I have vainly cherished for a number of years, namely that someone with some scientific equipment would carry forward the lines of enquiry which I suggested in *The Way of a Trout with a Fly*. I cannot give you the man's name at present, but I think he is on the right track, and I am only hoping that I shall stick it out long enough to see his success.

With K.R. and all good wishes,

Yours sincerely,
G.E.M. Skues

January 7, 1929

Dear La Branche,

I have ordered of the Thomas Rod Company for a friend of mine for delivery in good time for April a 9½ foot fly rod of the mahogany finish, with agate butt ring and agate top rings, and a Wells handle with space to carry a Hardy Perfect reel. I wonder whether you would be kind enough to test the rod and approve the action as being suitable for (dry & wet fly) the Itchen, not too hard on fine gut for that water or for some of the smaller waters of this country, or at any rate the waters where the fish run small. I have told Mr. Thomas I would ask you to handle the rod for me and see whether it is likely to suit. It is absolutely imperative that the rod should be over here in time for presentation by the wife to her husband on the occasion of their Silver Wedding in April next.

Mr. Thomas does'nt seem to have required any reference from me, but if he makes any enquiries as to my ability to pay for the rod, I suppose I may rely upon you to assure him that I am competent to pay up?

Christmas this year was extraordinarily mild, with the birds actually mating, and I spent the mornings of the 25th and 26th December in tying 3 dozen flies for the New Year.

I hope my article in the Bulletin on 'A Day's fishing on the Itchen' was regarded as having some interest for Americans.

K.R.
Yours ever,
G.E.M.S.

January 12, 1929
My dear La Branche,

Very many thanks for your letter of the 4th inst. I was assured that Mr. Thomas was considered a better man than Mills nowadays in New York. The type of rod I have ordered is one called 'Mahogany Finish' and I have asked that it should be stiff enough for dry fly, but not too hard on fine gut or so stiff as not to be good at hooking smaller fish that we get on the Itchen; that it should have agate ring on the butt and agate top rings properly protected, and the reel seat should be big enough to carry a Hardy Perfection reel.

It is very kind of you to take this trouble on my behalf. I much appreciate your kindness.

With regard to my name carrying sufficient weight, it does not by any manner of means follow that because a man writes on a subject, that his financial position makes him reliable as a customer. I could name a man very eminent in a certain sport (not fishing) out of whom his creditors found the utmost difficulty in extracting the amount of their claims.

With kind regards,
Yours sincerely,
G.E.M. Skues

February 7, 1929
My dear La Branche,

I wonder whether you could find out for me what sort of price MacMillans are selling my two books *Minor Tactics* and *The Way of a Trout* for in New York? According to my Publishers' account they only get about 3/6d. a copy for them, and I imagine that they sell at about 2-dollars in the States which is about three times that sum. I am not at all particularly pleased with Messrs. Adam & Chas. Black's arrangements for sale in the States. Not only do they get next to nothing for them but apparently Americans find it very difficult to buy over there.

Yours sincerely,
G.E.M.S.

February 15, 1929

My dear Skues:

Your last letter leaves me undecided as to whether or not you intended the rod manufacturer to send the rod to me for inspection. If it was your intention to do so, I am afraid that I will not be able to see it, as I am leaving for the South on Monday next on advice of my physician.

If my defection is going to interfere with the early delivery of the rod, it might pay you to cable Thomas and have him ship it direct to you. I feel quite certain from what I have learned from men who have used his rods, that he will undoubtedly send you just what you want, and that it will have quality. He would be particularly anxious in your case to make a good job, as it might open up an avenue for him which I think up to this time has been blocked by Leonard.

Will write you some of my bonefishing experiences from the South, if I have strength enough to pull one in.

The hectic Stock Market has left us all knocked out, and the game is not worth it, so I am going to rest for a long time from now on, or try to.

Yours faithfully,

April 9, 1929

Dear Skues:

Having just returned from bonefishing in Florida, where I have been for two months, without a stenographer, I hasten to acknowledge receipt of your two letters.

As soon as I can get in touch with the proper people I will find out how your book has been hidden by its publishers here, or why it brings a price which, while it is not as great as the book is worth, is more than the publishers agreed to sell it for. I believe to a certain extent, its higher price here is due to the duty. What this is I do not know.

At the present time there is little indication that I can get over before the middle or end of May, if at all. Family affairs, and a tremendous nervousness and activity in the stock market prevents me from considering seriously a period of protracted loafing. . . .

According to reports you have had some rather strenuous weather in Great Britain, but we Americans permit no other nation to outstrip us in anything, if we can prevent it, so that we have had some weather of our own.

It grieves me terribly to feel at the moment, that I am not likely to renew our nice friendship this year in the regular order of the last few years. There is of course, still a chance that I will be over, and I am now lending every effort to making it a go.

Please save a brace or two or your nice Itchen fish for me to practice on in the event that I am successful.

Always my warmest regards.

P.S. I have not seen Lord for months and have no knowledge of his plans. We have both been frightfully busy.

April 17, 1929
My dear La Branche,

It was pleasant to see your signature again. It is very kind of you to offer to enquire about why my books (not book) have not been freely dealt with by the Publishers in New York. It is not that I care particularly about the small amount which the books give me, but the Scot in me rather resents being left out in the distribution of the proceeds of my work to such an extent as I seem to have been.

I am sorry to hear that there is a possibility that you and Lord may not be coming over. I was looking forward to reserving you each a couple of days during the course of a week when the Mayfly was'nt on, and taking the time off to accompany you. The dates available for you and Lord, according to my guest weeks, would have been the 21st, 22nd, 23rd and 24th May.

. . . I am afraid that an invitation to Goodbody to fish, even during the Mayfly season this year, will not be a great privilege, as, (as you will see from my letter) we are suffering from a regular water famine from lack of winter rains. If one does'nt get the reservoirs of the chalk stored with water before the end of February, the season is bound to be a poor one, and I think this year is going to be worse than I have ever known it. I expect the big fish on my water will be uncatchable. Very likely lots of them will have dropped down to the Town water, with a chance of their falling victims to the local Town angler with a worm or maggots. . . .

Yours sincerely,
G.E.M. Skues

September 30, 1930
My dear La Branche,

. . .

I am sorry you have had such a hard time during the past year and have missed your fishing. I understand however that you have had some compensations, on which many congratulations.

My own fishing on the Itchen this year was poor up to the end of

July, although I got a good many trout, I had none up to 2 lbs, in fact none over 1 lb. 14 oz. all that time, and the fish as a whole ran small. In the first three week-ends of August however I had 7 two pounders up to 2 lbs. 7 oz. and a trout of 3 lbs 2 oz. This made me think that the big fish were probably there all the time, but for some reason or other not showing on the surface.

You will have gathered from the above account that I was not entirely incapacitated, but my shoulder is still a good deal restricted in action and it looks as if the doctor was right who said that probably I should never regain complete freedom.

Yours ever,
G.E.M. Skues

December 29, 1931
Dear La Branche,

Thank you very much for your Christmas reminder of your existence. I had not forgotten, though you have done your best by dropping your May–June visit to England to drop out of memory.

Your many friends over here, however, have not lost interest or given up hope of your early return. Lord's visit to the Itchen without you last June, though it was a pleasure to have him, seemed somehow incomplete.

Taverner has presented me with his book on Salmon Fishing, but it has been borrowed by friends that I have not yet had time to read even your Chapter on the dry fly for Salmon or "Woods on the Greased Line Method". Bostock, who fished with Wood on the Dee a year or two back and was greatly taken with his methods, had a rod on my length of the Itchen this last year, but is resigning owing to the stringency of the times. I am managing to hold on, and I hope that you will be over next Spring and that you will give me the pleasure of your company on the Itchen as in the past. I have been devoting most of my time on the river to developing nymph fishing and ascertaining the best patterns.

I don't know whether you have yet seen my friend Col. E.W. Harding's book *The Fly Fisher and the Trout's Point of View*? If you have not, do not fail to get it. It carries on a good deal further, and very ably, the examination of problems which baffled me in *The Way of a Trout with a Fly*. I am sure it will impress you.

With all good wishes for the New Year to you and yours.

Ever yours sincerely,
G.E.M. Skues

January 15, 1932

Dear Skues:

Your letter was a delightful surprise. I had wondered whether you had forgotten that I was still in the land of the living. I am, I am glad to say, though very much the worse for wear, due to the terrible battle we have all been in for the last two years.

How I envied Lord his trip with you to the Itchen. My recollections of your river and fishing with you will linger as long as my mind functions. I can even remember the fish we lost on the Kennet. I was sorry to lose this nice river, but I do not enjoy fishing among disagreeable people or in an uncharitable neighborhood.

A fishing on the Test was just offered me at a reasonable figure. It is just below the Houghton Club Water. Unfortunately, I cannot see my way clear to coming over this Spring. At least not at the moment, but if I do, I shall pay my respects to you immediately upon arrival.

Taverner's book is quite complete, although, I do not like the chapter on the "Dry Fly". Although I had promised to write on the subject for Mr. Taverner, it was impossible for me to find time, so I suggested that if he could not get anybody else to do it, he could take such material from my book as he thought would suit his purpose. This he did, but it appears to me quite distorted. However, nobody will know the difference.

I am now reading Col. Harding's book. It is most interesting and I am so glad that he gives you the high place in angling, which is yours.

My best regards to you, as always and with best wishes for the New Year, I am

The book referred to in the following letter would be *Sidelines, Sidelights and Reflections,* published in 1932.

May 25, 1932

My dear Skues:

At long last you have produced another book. I cannot wait to see it and I am presuming upon your good nature by asking you to sign your name on two copies, one for me and one for my son Robert, the small boy to whom you gave some flies in your office three or four years ago.

I am enclosing an order to the publisher together with the check for both copies. I would have sent the order direct, but I was fearful that they might miss getting your autograph and forward them without, which would have been dreadful for me.

I have just had a nice letter from John Hills announcing the *Further Chronicles* of the Houghton Club by R.P. Page, Esquire. I think I met Mr.

Page at Stockbridge when I was there with Hills, and I have sent for a copy of a book which I am sure must be interesting. Have you seen it?

You have no idea how tragic it is for me not to have been able to get over to see you this spring. Not only have I missed a day or two on your lovely river, but I have had to go through a grinding which has left little but a few bones. We may pull out of the hole, but some of us will find that it is already too deep at the bottom. Tell me how is your health, and what have you done on the Itchen, so far? I have had but two days, one blank and the other two half-pounders. Miserable days, both.

My best regards as always and best wishes for a heavy fish.
Yours faithfully,

June 3, 1932
My dear La Branche,

Many thanks for your birthday letter of the 25th May. I am sincerely sorry that you feel that you have arrived at the mature age of 110. It makes me feel that in my 74th year I am in my childhood—not second, I hope.

I will certainly sign the two copies of the new book for you when the Publishers send them along. But you were a bit rash in ordering them before knowing anything about the book. It is nothing but a collection of my old articles in the Fly Fishers Club *Journal* and a few other periodicals, and reading the proofs I felt thoroughly bored with them, and I had not expected any readers to be anything else.

I saw Major Hills last night with his young wife at a Dinner which was given by Owen Smith, the Prime Warden of the Fishmongers Company to 130 anglers including Lord Grey. I have seen the *Further Chronicles* of the Houghton Club. It is carried on very much on the same lines as the original *Chronicles,* but it is necessarily very little more than a 'scissors and paste' work. I also have met Page, the author, at the Houghton Club, on more than one occasion.

This year has not seemed to be quite normal in that I have not had either you or Lord or any of my other American friends down on my water.

It may interest you to know that Fraser has not the whole of the water that he used to have when he let rods to you and Lord, and that he has to be content to begin somewhere below Moon's Mill fishing from there down to the bottom.

The Itchen fishing has not been very satisfactory this year. I do not think I have ever known the fish more pernickety, and I have already had more than one blank day, and up to the present only one two pounder has been caught during the season. Last year I had several by this time and I killed 8½ brace during the season from 2lbs to

3lbs. I doubt whether the big fish have yet come out of their hides. We had one season, a few years ago, when they only showed for a week during the whole season, and then we saw that there was a fine stock of really big fish, for that water.

Apart from foot trouble, which rather restricts the pace of my getting about, I keep extraordinarily well.

I do not know whether you knew old Priddis, the keeper for so many years on Cox's water. I am sorry to get a letter to-day informing me that he died, after a short but painful illness, yesterday.

When you get my new book you will find a chapter in it about him under the title "Dabchick" the signature over which, for so many years, he reported the Itchen in the *Field*....

Yours sincerely,
G.E.M. Skues

June 30, 1932
My dear Skues:

Many thanks for troubling to inscribe the two books which have just reached me.

Glancing through the book hurriedly, I see no reason for your being bored with what you have done. I consider it a great contribution to angling literature, as I always so considered everything you have written. I will give you a further opinion when I finish reading it.

I am sorry to learn that Fraser has lost part of his water and while I found him to be rather irascible at times, I rather liked him. I was given to understand that he could easily be excused for being sour occasionally.

It is likely that St. George took the upper water as I suspected he would, notwithstanding the protestations he made to me that he only wanted the cottage and the garden. However, I may be able to find a bit of fishing if I am able physically and financially to undertake a trip to Great Britain next year....

It was sad news to hear of the death of your keeper, Priddis. I remember him well and his extreme modesty when you mentioned in his presence and mine, that he had been a champion swimmer. I shall read with interest what you have to say about him in the book....

Today we are in the throes of a political campaign for the Presidency in November. Politics is a game played here quite differently perhaps from the way it is played in Great Britain. Our politicians are out for individual gain and will say or do anything to get votes, frequently, against their own opinions and judgment on certain forms of legislation. Some of us feel that we are in a hopeless mess. I, for one, feel that a monarchy or dictatorship is our only salvation. It is quite possible that something of the sort may occur within the next fifty years—little consolation to us.

If anything of interest develops here, I will let you know. In the meantime, I get a little rest every day or two on nearby trout streams, without killing many large fish. I had the misfortune to lose a good three pounder the other day. I attribute the loss of this fish to the depression.

Thanks again for your courtesy and believe me, as ever
Yours faithfully,

September 21, 1933
My dear Skues:

It was so nice to see you again and I enjoyed tremendously the two days we had on the river together.

While I was grossly insulted by your fish, I did have great sport, though your keeper seemed mystified when I told him that I had had, but had killed no fish.

Sometime soon some oranges and grapefruit will reach your home. The oranges come from California and the grapefruit from Florida—the new crop. I hope you will like them.

When I can pull myself together and catch up the loose threads of business, I will get in touch with Adam and Charles Black and learn, if I can, what it would cost to produce an illustrated edition of *Minor Tactics*. In the meantime, if you are still in touch with them and feel like doing it, you might suggest the possibility of my becoming interested in the publication and perhaps save time in a negotiation. If you would rather not approach them, I will do it.

Again many thanks for your kindness to me and I hope that I will be able to see you again in the Spring.

As ever,

October 3, 1933
My dear La Branche,

I have heard from A & C Black Ltd., that they do not think there can be any objection to an illustrated American edition, and that they will write to you to that effect. When the book was first published they objected to my having a separate American edition. I should be interested to see what you propose in the way of illustrations.

Yours sincerely,
G.E.M.S.

December 29, 1934

My dear La Branche,

I have left my Christmas letter to you too long for it to reach you at the proper date, and the card from Mrs. La Branche and yourself puts me to shame. But I hope it is not too late to wish you a first-rate season in 1935, and all the other good fortune you could wish for yourself.

1934, though it produced quite a fair number of trout, and those in fine fighting fettle, was disappointing inasmuch as there was not a two-pounder caught on the length until after I knocked off at the end of August, and then only four—three being just over the 2 lbs., and one 2 lbs. 11 oz., the latter foulhooked.

We are having good autumn rains, so I hope the springs will fill up and give us a stream with some pace in it, instead of the sluggish, scarcely moving water of 1934, and I hope we may be seeing you over here at a seasonable time for a sling at our fish.

You may remember that I told you that I anticipated that my last book would be a flop. It has proved a flop all right. In the year ending 1st June last only 33 copies were sold, and I should not be surprised to find the publishers disposing of the balance for what they will fetch as remainders. I ought not to have let myself be pushed into permitting publication.

I daresay that you have seen that my good friend Colonel E.W. Harding (author of *The Flyfisher and the Trout's Point of View*) died in August last. He was hard at work almost to the last in preparations for another book, but his notes and material are in no shape to allow of their being completed and published by an Editor. It is a tragedy. His last paper I have had printed in the December *Salmon & Trout Magazine*.

H.S. Hall, inventor of the eyed hook for trout flies, also died in the year. He was an Original Member of the F.F.C., and though he saw the fiftieth year of the Club's existence, he did not live to see the fiftieth anniversary of the foundation. (18th December 1934) He was another old friend. At the age of 76 I find them dropping fast, and I fail to understand why I have been permitted to hang on. Harding was only 56.

I don't know whether you remember Dr. Barton. He is president of the F.F.C. for this year—and another very good friend of mine, and thank goodness is full of life and energy. He is also the Editor of the Club Journal, and a first-rate amateur photographer.

I am afraid that this is a dull and lugubrious letter. Please, with my best wishes for 1935 and on, accept the apologies of,

Yours sincerely ever,

G.E.M. Skues

The Jennings book referred to in the next letter is *A Book of Trout Flies,* published by Derrydale Press in 1935. It was to be regarded as the first book to do for American trout streams (a few northeastern ones, actually) what several British authors of the nineteenth century had done for their streams.

January 3, 1936
My dear La Branche,

I duly received from you and Mrs. La Branche your kind Christmas and New Year greeting. I hope it left you well and flourishing. Apart from some foot trouble, the legacy of an accident which I had years ago, I have little to complain of in the way of health.

I am glad to see that Eugene Connett III has at last got out his book by Jennings on American Trout Flies, and I am looking forward greatly to reading it when the F.F.C. gets a copy. The expense is a bit more than I like to run to in the present hard times.

With all good wishes,
Yours sincerely,
G.E.M. Skues

September 15, 1936
Mr dear La Branche,

You were a disappointment again this year in that you did not put in an appearance during the trout-fishing season. Lord was over, but I only saw him for an hour or so when he put in at the F.F.C. to have tea with me the day before he started on his return to the States. If you had come, however, I could not have done more for you in the way of fishing than invite you to share my rod, for owing to some mysterious failure of the last two or three spawning seasons our stock of trout ran most astonishingly low and the members of my syndicate decided there must be no guest days, though a member fishing might share his rod with a guest. As a consequence of the failure of stock the trout which were caught ran an extraordinarily good size. I caught few under 1½ lbs. and I had ten brace from 2 lbs. to 2 lbs. 15 oz., including five over 2¾ lbs. These fish were in magnificent fettle and put up splendid fights. Trout of 14 inches would weigh 1 lb. 9 oz., and 1 lb. 10 oz.; 15 inches 2 lbs. and 15 inches 2½ lbs. Conditions have been in many respects like the years following the war, during the latter years of which (owing to the calling up of the Keepers) pike increased enormously and ate us out of house and home. In those years, as in the last two, the grayling almost disappeared, but I have not seen any evidence of big pike. If you have a copy of my last book

Side Lines, you will be able to read in the chapter "An Itchen Retrospect" what happened then. My colleagues are very gloomy about the future; but I remember how quickly the river recovered and that 1921 was one of the best years we had ever had. *Side Lines*, by the way, continues to be (as I prophesied it would) a flop. Only 40 copies selling in the year ending 1st June last, and only 18 in the year before—as against 373 copies of *The Way of a Trout*, which was first published in 1921 and had had plenty of time to be forgotten.

Our water is threatened with another tragedy. A bye pass road is being constructed to pass between the river and the railway line on the upstream side of the line. Incidentally it will destroy the Spinney and it will be difficult, in casting across stream, to prevent one's line passing over the road and hooking pedestrians, cyclists and motor cars. Privacy will, of course, be gone and trespassers will have easy access to our banks. It is difficult enough to keep them out as it is.

The F.F.C. has been having a period of ill-luck. It has lost its last two Presidents, Dr. J. Brunton Blaikie and Harry Plunket Greene (the singer) during their years of office after abdominal operations, and my good friend Dr. Barton, the previous president, went down on the day following the end of his Presidency with acute inflammation of the gall bladder, involving its extirpation. Thank goodness he has made a good recovery and is managing in his retirement to put in a good deal of fishing on a variety of friendly waters.

I continued through the first part of my season to study the dressing of nymphs to represent those which I found in the crops of my fish, but about the middle of the season I was rather startled to receive an appeal from my colleagues not to go on nymph fishing on the ground that it was not flyfishing, and because the stock was so low; and as I did not like to pursue a practice disapproved of by my colleagues, I gave up nymphs for the season. I found, however, that as the fish continued their subaqueous feeding it was necessary to sink my fly, so I didn't see much point in the objection. A Mr. C.E. Pain, who wrote a book called *Fifty years on the Test* tells me that nymph fishing is now practised on that river from Overton (near the source) to the sea.

Barton is off next week to fish Fraser's water at Ramsbury. I have not been there for years, though I have been asked by both Fraser and St. George, because I know that if I accepted the invitation of one I should offend the other. It is a great pity.

I entered on my 79th year in mid-August, so if you are to see me again you should pay another visit to the old country next year. Meanwhile, Ave,

Yours very sincerely,
G.E.M. Skues

January 6, 1937

Dear Skues:

Your delicately subtle compliment warmed the cockles of my heart. There was just a chance last Spring that I could have come over with Lord and really hoped to but at the last moment I had to give up the idea.

It is sad to hear of the distressing conditions on your water. The thing that would annoy me most if I were a member of your syndicate, would be the building of the bye pass to come so close to the stream and destroying the Spinney. I think that the failure of the trout to spawn could be remedied by introducing some new blood or by restocking but there is nothing that can be done to keep people from tresspassing and perhaps even poaching.

Your fish were indeed excellent and of course nothing like that record can be had on any of our rivers. In early June I killed a fish 20½ inches long which, while apparently in good condition and a very strong fish, weighed 3 lbs. The few others that I took were hardly worth mentioning and all were returned to the river. My usual fishing in August which I consider the best of the season, was nil. This was due to the fact that for six weeks we had had not a single drop of rain and the rivers went down lower than I have ever seen them. Some fish were to be seen in the pools but one had not the heart to fish for them, they looked so distressed and fearful. Nature certainly had it in for the angler last year. In early May we had a tremendous flood which spread the rivers beyond their banks making deep lakes in the adjoining fields and when the torrents subsided the fish were left to die all through the meadows and nothing could be done to save them except perhaps a few fish. This flood in May and the draught in July particulary, killed off the fish in our brooks for the next two or three years.

If I am to have any fly fishing I may have to come to England and spend a week or so on the Gloucestershire Colne at Fairford with perhaps a quick trip into Wales. You may rest assured that if I do come I shall give myself the pleasure of having you to dinner with me one night with perhaps Jack Hills and Laurence Dunne.

I am glad to learn that our good friend Dr. Barton has made such a good recovery. I heard a bit earlier that he was getting along splendidly.

Why *Side Lines* should be doing so badly, I cannot tell nor do I understand why you prophecied that it would be a flop. I think it is a great book. My opinion, given for what it is worth, is that its title does not indicate to the average fisherman that it is a book on angling. It would be interesting to see what would happen if the book could be brought out under another title. Of course, the best book that was ever written is *Minor Tactics* with *The Way of a Trout* not far behind. . . .

We are leaving tomorrow for my annual bonefishing which is merely one way of getting into a warm climate.

Hoping the New Year will be full of health and happiness for you, I am Yours as always,

January 19, 1937
Dear La Branche,

I was more than pleased to get your letter of the 8th instant. I hope you may be able to come to England in 1937 and to be able to have you down on the Itchen for a couple of days in May or June. It would be a temptation to take a Monday and Tuesday off when no one is likely to be on the water and you could use my rod.

I don't like your plan of "new blood or restocking". Quite apart from the fact that furunculosis is often introduced by the infusion of new blood or restocking, the splendid quality of our home-bred stock would certainly be lowered. We were offered Itchen bred fish from upstream, but I found that 14 inch fish only weighed 1 lb. 4 oz against our home-breds 1 lb. 10 oz.

I am sorry you had so poor a 1936 season. I have seen flood water on the Test at Bransbury Common with the fish swimming about among the grass; but nearly all were netted and returned by the keepers.

It is kind indeed of you to suggest entertaining me along with Jack Hills and Laurie Dunne, but don't do it on the Ritz scale. I suppose you know that Dunne is now a Metropolitan Magistrate.

Hills has just recently (December) published a new book called *My Sporting Life* (Philip Allan 12/6) which it might interest you to have. *Side Lines* is a poor title—but at the moment I could not think of a better, nor have I done so since. Can you suggest an improvement? . . .

K.R. and all good wished for 1937 et seq.
Yours ever,
G.E.M. Skues

October 7, 1938
My dear La Branche,

Now that my fifty-sixth (and I am afraid my last) Itchen season has come to its inevitable end I am feeling that I have long neglected writing to you. Indeed, it seems as if you and Lord and other kind American friends (other than the faithful Boies) had been slipping away from us for some years past. I suppose that as the years slip by all this is in the way of nature and I passed my eighth decade in mid-August.

I have had a little correspondence with John Alden Knight on his Solunar theory (in which, though I don't profess to follow it or to be quite convinced by it, I do not feel he has had quite the square deal he is entitled to) but apart from him and Connett and Boies I have not heard anything from your side the streak for a long while.

Not long since I heard from Howard St. George. He has left Harbrook and given up fishing, and his part of the Ramsbury water and Harbrook have been let to a stranger to me—some name like Underdown or Underwood—and Fraser is still out of it. He has not been seen much at the Club for some time past. Barton has fished his water, but I have had nothing to take me in that direction for years past.

Latterly my Itchen colleagues have developed strict dry fly principles (if that be the right word) and have expressed strong dispproval of my excursions in the direction of fishing the artificial nymph and I, disliking the idea of fishing under conditions of disapproval on the part of my colleagues and, indeed, not expecting to be fit enough after turning 80 to go on for another season, resigned my rod from the end of this season.

The justice of the attitude of my colleagues may be inferred from the fact that during 1936 I took 18 two-pounders (up to 2 lbs. 14 oz) besides a number of smaller fish of which only one was under 1½ lbs, and that of the two-pounders two only took a floating fly and two only under that weight did so while scarcely a fish whose stomach contents I examined (which included all the two-pounders) had a winged dun among them, and apart from shrimps, an occasional blue bottle and beetle and a sedge or two there was nothing but nymphs in them. The quality of the Itchen trout has been magnificient, a 14 inch fish (in most waters 1½ lbs) would run 1 lb. 9 oz. or 1 lb. 10 oz., a 15 inch fish 2 lbs., a 16 inch fish 2½ lbs. and I ony caught one 17 inch fish in the season, an old cock fish of 2¾ lbs. Of course, I did my best (generally successfully) to avoid catching fish under 1½ lbs. Latterly the trout became very careful, so that one day I rose 21 fish and only hooked one, and he got off in the weeds.

Bostock (one of our members) caught a perfectly magnificent 3½ pounder during the evening rise. It was only 1½ inches longer than a really beautiful 2¼ pounder which fell to my rod the same evening. It was more like a Thames trout than a normal Itchen fish and was quite the finest fish I ever saw taken from the Itchen— much finer than one of 3 lbs. 14 oz which I had out last year. . . .

Between ourselves I may mention that I have on the stocks a small book on the subject of Nymph fishing in Chalk Streams which should come out early next year. The Publishers will be Adam & Chas. Black.

During 1937 my colleagues were very unhappy about the lowness of our stock of trout, but 1938—though it began by being no better—by the middle of the season gave strong proof of the recovery which I had prophesied of it, and I expect my colleagues will find next year that the river is as good as ever.

Bostock had a week in July or August on the Test at Leckford where, by reason of stocking with big fish, big baskets are obtained, and says that compared to the Abbots Barton trout the Test fish come in when hooked like so many pieces of string.

I hope all this, if you get so far, will not have bored you to extinction.

I should like, when you can spare the time to write, to have news of yourself and particularly to hear that there is a prospect of you (and Lord) coming over next year—though I shall not, alas, be able to give you (as I should like) a welcome on the Itchen.

With very K.R.,
Cordially yours,
G.E.M. Skues

October 20, 1938
My dear La Branche,

Your letter of the 13th instant reached me this morning and I am extremely sorry to hear that I missed you on your visit and also that you were laid up for most of the short time you were here.

I knew Hills had had an operation and had had to have a subsequent operation. I wrote to him a little while ago saying I hoped he had got over it, but have had no reply and I expect your letter explains why. I am very sorry he is ill as he is a very good friend. He has fished with me on several occasions and on one I was his guest at the Houghton Club for a week-end in July [.] He mentions the occasion in his last book. I have lost so many friends of late years through operations that I am fearful for him. . . .

Yours sincerely,
G.E.M. Skues

April 4, 1939
My dear La Branche,

. . .

I will be very pleased to inscribe one copy of my Nymph fishing book for your library. I expect the Publishers will be sending it to me to be signed up before dispatch. I have signed a number of copies for various friends, including one for Hunt.

I do not quite understand what you mean by your enquiry "what have I to take back". I do not apologise for anything or recant anything. I was not greatly pleased with the title myself, but I couldnot think of anything that would at once call attention to the subject and be an improvement on the title selected. I have had several very friendly reviews, and one or two sour ones—particulary one from *Game & Gun*. *The Field*, however, said that I had doubled the pleasure and interest of chalkstream fishing.

Yes: it was very sad about poor Hills; but he was told not long before he died that his name was in the Honors List and I think he knew that if he did not survive the Title would go to his son as if he had been in the List. I had been lookiing forward for some time to Hills' getting better and fishing with me before the last season ended. It was only quite latterly that I realised that I would have to give up that hope....

Yours sincerely,
G.E.M. Skues

It would probably take considerable enterprise and a little luck to find out if the calendar proposed by Doris Bennion in the following letter was published, and if it contained the quotation that La Branche provided, which immediately follows her letter.

Sunnyside Residential Hotel,
York Road,
Parktown,
Johannesburg.
South Africa.

August 18, 1939
G.M.L. La Branche, Esq.,
50 Broadway,
New York.
Dear Sir,

Mr. G.E.M. Skues, of London, England, has very kindly given me your name, and I am writing to ask you if you would send me a fishing quotation (with source names) to be included in an Anglers' Quotations Calendar I am getting together.

Either a short piece of prose or a verse or an original saying would be suitable, and my idea is to have the words—Contributed by —after each quotation.

I should be very much obliged for this courtesy.
Yours faithfully,
(Mrs.) Doris Bennion.

[La Branche quotation:]

It is doubless true that the fly fisher derives no small part of his pleasure from the act of selecting and purchasing flies. It is within the experience of every fly fisher, I think, that, under the influence of the memory of a certain fish taken on a particular pattern of fly, he includes a dozen or two of the sort in his next purchase. Perhaps the fly is a nondescript that he may never again find successful, but, nevertheless, he adds it to his store. Angling friends recommend their patterns to him, or some special flies they found taking under certain circumstances or over particular streams, and these, too, he buys and puts away. Maybe he may never use one of them, and in the end he comes, perhaps, to feel, as does the philatelist, great pleasure in the possession of a worthy collection: he has the pride of ownership, but no thought of putting his treasures to use. Of course, there can be no reasonable objection to fly collecting, and I can see how it may become as fascinating an employment as stamp or coin collecting.

For those not familiar with the jargon, a "brace" of fish is two. Note also Skues' disparaging remark about the flies in the book by "Roy Bergman." This is apparently a reference to Ray Bergman's book *Trout* (1938), which contained several color plates of traditional American wet flies. Though those often gaudy and nonimitative flies were out of favor with imitationists like Skues, they were still quite popular with many American fishermen, probably because they still worked.

January 2, 1940
My dear La Branche,

. . .

I imagine that it is unlikely that you will be paying a visit to this country while this cock-eyed war continues.

I am in my 82nd year and my memory is not quite what it was, so I do not know whether I had told you that I resigned my rod on the Itchen at the end of the 1938 season. I did so with extreme regret, but in view of the dry fly purism of my colleagues (leading them to regard my practice of nymph fishing as unfair and unsportsman-like) I did not feel that I could go on with them in an atmosphere of disapproval and on sufferance, though I do not believe they would ever have asked for my resignation.

There seems to have been latterly a recrudescence of dry fly intolerance, and that and a certain resentment at having to give up fishing a river I had been fishing for 56 years, led me in the autumn of 1938 to put my views as to the theory and practice of nymph fishing into a small volume *Nymph Fishing for Chalk Stream Trout* which was published in February 1939 by A. & C. Black, Ltd. I have not yet heard what sale it has had, but no doubt the impending war threat did it no good. It had a fair but not unanimous press.

In order not to be without a fishing I took a rod on the Nadder near Wilton (it runs into the Wiltshire Avon just below Salisbury) and I fished it most week-ends from the middle of April to the outbreak of war on the 1st September.

It proved nothing like as good a river as the Itchen, my last season on which brought me 18 two-pounders up to 2 lb. 14 oz. half of them 2½ lb. and upwards, in addition to a number of fish from my personal 1½ lb. limit up to 1 lb. 15 oz. These fish were beautifully short and thick. 14 inches weighed 1½ lb., 15 inches 2 lb., 16 inches 2½ lb. and so on. There were a few biggish trout in my part of the Nadder, but none of such high quality. I had five from 2 lb. 2 oz. to 3 lb. 3 oz. and my brother had a three-pounder. So had one other rod. But there was a poor stock of medium sized fish from 1½ lb. to 2 lb. and none too many younger stock coming along. The grayling were numerous but small—best 1¼ lbs. Still it was better than nothing.

If I had only known it I might have had a rod on the Wylye, a much better river and a true chalk stream, which the Nadder is not.

There is Mayfly on the Nadder, but it behaved most queerly. Though there were a few—very few—hatching every day I was on the water from 12th May to 1st September including the fortnight which would normally cover the Mayfly season I never saw one taken by a trout.

I was tempted to take the rod by my experience of a length two or three miles upstream which I had before the previous war. In three days in late May I caught no less than 54 brace of which 44 brace took the sunk Alder, 8 brace Mayfly and 2 brace Red Quill. I only kept 3½ brace—none quite 2 lbs.

I also had some good sport on the same length with the B.W.O. And it was there that I made the discovery of the virtues, when the trout were nymphing at B.W.O., of the pattern described as "Occasionally it" at p.234 of *Side Lines*.

I had to take the Nadder Rod for 1940 as well. So I have to pay for a season during which, if the war lasts, as I expect it will, I shall be unable to make normal use of it. But I hope to be able to induce my landlord to let me give leave to Naval and Military men for a few days at a time. Under existing conditions I have to accompany any guest....

I don't think you know Major J. Waller Hills, M.P., the author of *A Summer in the Test, A History of Fly fishing for Trout,* and other books. He died last year much regretted. His brother Col. Hills had the Ramsbury water before Fraser, and Hills used to fish it. He writes about it in his last Volume *My Sporting Life*. I do not suppose I shall ever see that water again. Dr Barton has had leave in it from Fraser fairly frequently—but when Fraser and St. George fell out, I refused invitations from both so as not to give offence to the other. . . .

Eugene V. Connett III sent me recently a book of his called *Random Casts*. In it I was delighted to find that he (with the aid of some of your men of science) had carried quite a bit further the investigation of problems connected with the vision of the Trout which I examined in *The Way of a Trout* with a fly and of which I made certain tentative solutions. It is pleasing to find that Connett's book did not displace any of these.

Connett had previously presented me with a copy of Preston Jenning's book on American Trout Flies also published by him. I was delighted to see that something genuine was being done on your side of the damp to displace the garish fancy flies of the older books (and Roy Bergman's) with patterns based on natural insects. Connett's books are beautifully turned out, but naturally quite expensive.

I hope you will not have been bored by this long screed. After all you probably possess a waste paper basket.

Nevertheless if you can find time to drop me a line to tell me how things are with you I shall be grateful.

Every morning when I wake the first thing to meet my eyes is your portrait on the wall at the foot of my bed.

Believe me with K.R. and all good wishes for the New Year and on.

Yours as ever
G.E.M. Skues

Possibly in part because he never was able to stop defending nymph fishing from the dry-fly purists, Skues never stopped hammering on Halford, whose dry-fly theories were regularly invoked against him almost to the day of his death.

February 27, 1940
Dear La Branche,

Borrowing the other day from my friend Eric Taverner a snapshot which he took of me two or three years ago fishing the main river of the Winnal length of Itchen, I had a few enlargements made, and I am enclosing you one in case you care to paste it into your copy of one of my books.

You may be interested to learn that Howard St. George who rented from Sir Francis Burdett Coutts the part of the Kennett above Moons Mill in succession to R.A. Fraser died a few days back at Bournemouth, aged 82. I remember his coming up to watch you and me fishing Mayfly in the Meadow below Moons Mill the last season you had a rod on the Kennett.

Both he and Fraser used to invite me to fish but I felt that if I accepted the invitation of either I should only be giving offence to the other. I always have felt that Fraser had rather a raw deal when Burdett only renewed his lease for part of the water below Moons Mill, for he had spent lavishly on the house in the expectation of a renewal.

If [it] was, as you of course know, the water which Halford . . . rented in the Nineties, in respect of which Halford wrote that deplorable book, *Making a Fishery*. A client of mine who owned some water lower down the Kennett borrowed the book and following the instructions of Halford destroyed the length (where his trout averaged 3lbs) so that the pike got them all and for years no trout were taken there.

After Halford's tenancy, Major J. Waller Hills (who wrote several angling books including *History of Fly fishing for Trout*) fished the Ramsbury water mainly as a guest of his brother Colonel Eustace Hills until the Colonel died in 1922. It was after that I think that Fraser took the water.

I am hoping to have a short holiday on the Nadder (Nr, Wilton) this season about Mayfly time in late May and early June, if not previously Hitled [Hitlered?] into smithereens. In any case I imagine 1940 will be my last season as I am in my 82nd year.

With K.R.
As ever,
Yours,
G.E.M. Skues

May 14, 1940
Dear Skues:

While I am a notoriously poor corresondent I did not fail to acknowledge receipt of your letter of February 27th which reached me in Florida on March 19th, a week after its arrival.

The photograph you enclosed is really a portrait and I am delighted with it and appreciate greatly your thought in sending it to me. I am inclined not to take your suggestion to paste it in a copy of one of your books which for a moment intrigued me. I prefer, however, to have it properly mounted and framed and hang it with some photographs I have of famous anglers and sportsmen including Arthur Wood, Ambrose Manell, Jack Hills and a few others. I hope you have no objection but I do not like the idea of having it buried in a book which might be preserved while I live, but could easily be neglected or destroyed afterward.

Our mutual friend, Kienbusch, telephoned me a few days ago saying that you had asked whether I had died or was sunk. From this I understood that you had not received my letter. Handling the post these days is a difficult matter. While letters from England reach here with fair regularity, one never knows from this side whether his letter arrives or not. None of our boats go over and there is no way of directing the transmission of a letter by any special steamer. To save delay and assuring you of my appreciation again, I am sending this letter by air post which apparently is swift and prompt. I would be glad to have you note the date of arrival of this letter so that we may know just how long a letter is in transit. . . .

I shall always remember the days we spent on your water at Winchester and particularly our day on the Kennet where together we lost a big fish. It saddens me to know that you had to give up the water on the Itchen you loved so well but I hope that the trout in the Nadder will be kind to you.

My best wishes.

July 11, 1941
Dear Skues:

Just another short line to you hoping that you will send me word that you are in fine fettle and having some good fishing on the Nadder.

We have no fishing here this year to speak of. We have had no rain since March and the rivers are practically dry except in one or two outlying districts.

I earnestly hope that none of Hitler's bombs come any way near you and from the looks of things from this side he has less chance now than he ever had of making it more disagreeable. We are rushing things to Great Britain in rapidly increasing quantities and it seems quite apparent that we will soon add physical assistance notwithstanding the fact that we wish to keep out of the war—that is, some of us.

It may seem lighthearted and gay to you during these horrible times to be going north with Dick Hunt to Canada for some salmon fishing—but I am leaving today for two weeks.

It may be my last chance to get there as by the time the season rolls around next year I may be helping with a gun somewhere.

Nothing would give me greater pleasure than to prove that Americans are good shots.

With all best wishes I am
Ever affectionately yours,

Nadder Vale Hotel, Wilton, Wilts., Eng.
July 22, 1941
Dear La Branche
It was very pleasant to me to receive your friendly letter of the 11th inst. which reached me this morning. As regards my 'fettle' I dont think that I ought to complain considering my age (83 as near as makes no difference) When I retired & came here in June 1940 I expected to finish my trout season in 1940 & to die in the winter or at best not to be fit for another season—but I am out in the water most days—I have had 3 trout of 2lbs 9oz each; several more two pounds to 2¼ lb. & a string from 1½ lbs to 1 lb 15 oz. Early in June the weeds had grown so thick that in many places they covered the river with flower beds from bank to bank. So though I hooked several big fish since I have mostly lost them in the weeds. So long as the weeds are under water only there is hope of getting a good fish out—but where they are right out of the surface it is a pretty hopeless job.
Your sympathy & that of your people generally & their practical help are much appreciated over here.
Yes it was bad luck the F.F.C. getting bombed. The Committee have declaimed the lease....
I am surprised to hear that your fishing this year has been so poor. Baird C. Foster from whom I hear from time to time seems to have had some good sport. We had a wet winter which looked like keeping our chalkstreams in fly all the summer—but it was followed by a spring which though cold right into June, was rainless & the Nadder has been lower than I have seen it. There came a wet 15 July (St. Swithuns) but no 40 days rain.

With all good wishes
As ever cordially yours
G.E.M. Skues

December 15, 1941
Dear Skues:
   ...
I hope your nice little fishing continues to be good. Our own has been very bad owing to lengthy droughts. I did, however, have two

good days with Dick Hunt on the Brodhead in Pennsylvania where we took the limit (10 fish) from 1¼ lbs. to 2¼ lbs. All were returned to the water with the exception of the largest fish. My salmon fishing was interrupted after being on the river in Canada for two days by the news that my wife had to undergo an emergency operation. I got back to town hurriedly and am glad to report that the operation was completely successful and she is now much better than she has been in a long time.

As always,

January 1, 1942
My dear La Branche

. . .

I heard the other day from Zerlock (one of the Little Itchen Syndicate) that the three members who remained after my resignation in 1938 have given up Winnal fishing as from the end of Dec. This insufficient stock—who I don't credit—for I walked up the Main from Darks Nest Spinney to the big Ry bridge in June 1940 & all along there were fine trout lying out & sucking in the nymphs greedily. A better plan wd have been that a Catchment Board is to be established for Test & Itchen. It horrifies me to think of this treatment of my dear old Itchen, having seen the godforsaken mess which the Avon [?] Board have made of the Wylye & the lower Nadder.

I suppose I am marooned here for the duration if I so long live as there seems no possibility under present conditions of finding a small place to suit me. I like the neighbourhood, the country & the air & I have made a few pleasant friends so I sh'nt mind much if it were not that I am unable to renew my rod on the adjoining length of the Nadder—a new leasee of the fishing have no room for me. I feel it rather rough luck for last year when he was not renewing his rod for 1941 I offered him as many days as he want subject only to them not being already pledged to another when he notified me. I have however a rod which gives me 30 days betw 30 April & 1st Oct for self & guest—so I shall not be entirely bereft. That rod here was in on the part muddled by the Catchment Board.

Dr Barton whom you may remember at the F.F.C. has lately published a successful volume of Reminiscences *A Doctor Remembers* & he has an angling book with his publishers, to come out as soon as circumstances will permit.

Not having been up to Town since I came here in June 1940 I have rather lost touch with the F.F.C. & so have no news of the members for you. It has just gone into new premises at the Junior Carleton as a temporary measure. . . .

Believe me Yours as ever,
G.E.M. Skues

January 1, 1942
My dear La Branche

. . .

Did I tell you that the three members of my Itchen Syndicate whom I left when my resignation took affect at the end of Aug 1938 have given up the fishing. So ends a long & for me a good period. I cannot afford to take on the water—& even if I could I do not think the climate of Winchester can suit me as a permanency. Fishing only at Weekends I found it fatiguing enough. The Wiltshire air suits me much better & I have had long days on the meadows with no more fatigue than a whiskey & soda would banish.

Yours as ever
G.E.M. Skues

April 9, 1944
Dear La Branche,

I heard the other day from your compatriot R. Carley Hunt & his mention of having had a recent conversation with you brought home to me that I have been very remiss in postponing writing you for so long. I have been here since my retirement in June 1940 & am now 2/3rd of the way through my 86th year. I still have a rod on the Nadder but fear that I am unlikely to make much use of it in the coming season which starts 1st May. When I came here in 1940 I could walk the 4 miles into Salisbury & the 4 miles back without undue fatigue, but that is now a bit beyond me. Last season I found 5 hours on the water with a bus ride there & back were fatiguing enough. The winter has produced a minimum of rain and as a result of that & the policy of the Catchment Board in rushing every drop of water to the sea without loss of a moments time results in the Nadder being 18 inches below Summers level as it was before the Board started the damnable dredging. So I don't expect 1944 to be much of a season anyhow. I hoped that last year wd have brought me a few members of the N.Y.A. Club to whom I could have given some of my days on the river, but only one (Col Jno Carlin[?]) turned up & I am not expecting many more this year. I miss my visits to the F.C.C. but I have 2 members & 1 ex member fishing down here whom I meet from time to time.

You may have heard that a factory at Newbury let some poison (prussic acid I understand) into the Kennet, poisoning many thousands of fish. Newbury is low enough down for the poison to have spared the best trout fishing. Below Newbury the trout seldom rise except to the Mayfly.

I see from the list of F.C.C. members that R. Atkin Fraser is no longer a member. I do not know whether he is retired or dead. Howard St. George who followed him on the Ramsbury upper water died some years ago. I do not think you know Major John Waller Hills M.P. whose brother had that water before Fraser. Hills wrote an interesting but not entirely accurate book on *The History of Fly Fishing*— & a quite charming book *A Summer on the Test* & another called *River Keeper*, a biography of old Lunn of the Houghton club— Both Hills and Lunn are dead. I dont understand how I came to be hanging on so long. . . .

You might be amused to hear that I have found my 3 books published by Black & priced on publication at 7/6 [,] 7/6 & 10/6 respectively selling in Salisbury (2nd hand of course at 21/- a piece & a correspondent complained that he was asked by an E[?] Bookseller £2.15 for *The Way of a Trout with a Fly*—Blacks are sorry they did not reprint. . . .

I do not known whether I ever thanked you for sending R.C. Hunt to me. He is quite delightful & so all the members of the F.F.C. who met him agreed.

With all good wishes
Cordially yours
G.E.M. Skues

June 29, 1944
Dear Skues:

Nothing could have pleased me more than to have received your letter of the 9th of April. It took a long time coming here. I have had it but a few days.

Am so sorry to hear that you have no means of transportation to your water on the Nadder. Perhaps now that the big push is on and going well, too, you may find it a bit easier. Four miles each way is a task for any one. I am considerably younger than you are although I feel twenty years older. I know that I could not do it and certainly, would not do it with the fishing here as poor as it is. Have not wet a line for two years and this year I had hoped to have an occasional half day on the river but a great drought we had this spring has practically ruined most of the brooks. . . .

I cannot understand how such a terrible thing could happen to the Kennet at Newbury. At least, poison cannot run up stream so I imagine that the Ramsbury water would not be affected, nor the river at Hungerford. Of course, prussic acid is deadly and I do not know whether this was the result of some factory spew or whether it was perpetrated by some miscreants. Anyhow, it is tragic.

Thanks for letting me know about Doctor Barton's book. I must get a copy of it. It must be well done. Besides being an expert angler he is a master photographer.

You mentioned the death of Major John Waller Hills. I know that he died just before Christmas, 1938, as I went over to see him in October of that year. I have the honor to be Godfather to his son, Sir Andrew Ashton Waller Hills. Jack Hills was a fine sportsman and a very knowledgeable man. I was extrememly fond of him and his death left a vacancy in my heart....

It is no surprise to me that £2.15. is offered for *The Way of a Trout with a Fly*. I imagine that *Minor Tactics* is unobtainable at any price. A recent book has been published here by Houghton, Mifflin & Company called *Under the Bridge*. The writer is Mr. Ferris Greenslet whom, I believe, is head of the firm. In it he mentions your name and described your book as "a classic of English angling literature". Curiously enough he mentioned my name too but with no such prominence.

I am so glad that you and all the members of the F.F.C. liked my friend Dick Hunt. He has been my fishing companion for years and if the Lord is good to me I am hoping to steal a week later on on his river in New Brunswick (Restigouche) for a try at a late run of salmon. Up to now the fishing has been very poor. The drought has affected even that section of the country.

You may be pleased to know that I have followed your advice and placed the very fine photograph, which you sent me, in one of your books. I feel certain, too, as you do, that a framed picture does not last long when an estate is disbursed. I am presenting this book to The Anglers Club of New York where it will have a home, at least, for a much longer period of time than any other that I could think of.

My best wishes as always.

December 20, 1945

My dear La Branche:

An account in the Bulletin by Colonel John Easton of his Mayfly day on the Kennett sent my memory back to the weekend on that water when I was a guest of yourself & F.B. Lord & to my often regretted clumsiness with the landing net which lost you a good fish—And of course I recall your visiting the Itchen with me & various incidents thereon. I am wondering whether, now that the war is over, conditions will improve enough to bring you & Lord & R.C. Hunt & others of my American friends over while I am still a going concern. I am in my 88th year & I think the past season has brought me to the end of my flyfishing & fly tying days. The Nadder on which I have had a rod since 1938 has, since the Catchment Board got to work on it in 1942, grown progressively more & more hopeless & I have resigned my rod & see myself unable to offer my friends any sport & reduced to taking my pleasure in reading & writing about it without practicing it. My hands have for the past year been too shaky for competent flydressing—And you see what the same trouble has made of my hand writing.

With kindest regards & all good wishes for 1946 & many years to come.
Yours as ever,
G.E.M.Skues

November 9, 1946
My dear La Branche
This morning has brought me a line from Dr. Barton telling me that Blacks had received from you an order for a copy of his very attractive *Album of the Chalkstreams* with a request that he should autograph the copy for you. So I infer that you are still going strong & keeping up your interest in the most interesting game in the world. I resigned my rod on the Nadder at the end of 1944 & gave up fly dressing since my hands became too shaky—but my interest is unabated. Seeing that my brother, though a keen & good angler with the fly, does not want to succeed to my angling library when I pass on—which, as I am in my 89th year, cannot be a very distant date, I have been dispensing of my angling library by degrees. I got £2.7/— for a copy of *Minor Tactics*—first pubd at 3/6 & later eds at 7/6—£3.7 for a copy of *The Way of A Trout with a Fly*—and the fly dressing interests dealer M— wrote me that he had refused £5 and more for his copies of both books & could have got £10 net. Scanty prices of course—as Blacks (who own the copyright outright) left reprinting new editions too late & then the paper supply ran out. But these prices are not unique. A year or two back the *Times* advertised an offer of £32 for a de luxe copy of *Brook & River Trouting* by two Bradford (Yorkshire) Anglers (Edmonds & Lee)—but at that time I was not selling. *Between ourselves* these authors wanted me to write them an introduction—but I wd not. Instead I made them lick into shape their somewhat deplorable English—for their knowledge & practice was quite good & they presented me with a copy of their deLuxe Ed with all their flies & the materials used in panels. The selling price was then the £4.4.—

So 32 is something of an offer.

Bartons book is selling like hot cakes. The publication day is the 12th inst. & Barton wrote me under date the 7th inst. that already over 3000 of the 4700 copies printed had been sold. The book of his 47 pictures is called *Wind in the Willows*. It formed the frontispiece of my 3rd book *Side Lines* & shows the bit of the Itchen side stream just below where the best "piscatorilus sacrum" used to be with me seated on the bank preparing to cast toward the trunk which carried the water from the main across the sidestream to water the meadows on the N. side of the river. It was not far below that point that on a gusty windy day you caught your first Itchen trout—a 2lber if I recollect right—on a rather large Sedge fly.

The Nadder which runs close behind this little hotel, has gone to bits as a trout river & as a grayling water too, since the local Catchment Board got to work on it. If it is not '[?]' as well as '[?]' I shd be interested to see a better explanation. The mischief extends far up the river. In the 1st decade of this century I had a Whitsuntide visit of 3 days on a stretch of water & waded some 4 miles or so upstream & caught 104 trout (84 on [?]) keeping 3½ brace & in May 1939 (before the Catchment Board got to work) my friend, Lamoin Birch, the Royal [?], in 4 days took 91 trout. Now an angler who gets a brace there has done pretty well.

While down here I have had some correspondence with a Scotch angler (N.J. Laurie by name) who is I think likely to make his mark as an angling writer. My nymph fishing book is confined to the Chalkstream. He is making a close study of nymph fishing on the rough rivers of the North. I should like to see what he makes of it but do not expect to last long enough.

Then there is a man named Monkhouse who was over on yr side some months ago & was a visitor at the Anglers Club of New York where you may possibly have met him. He is something & a big man in the Kodak Co. and is likely sooner or later to make quite a mark (with the aid of Kodachrome). Monkhouse is able on the subject of trout flies & their dressings. So keep your eye peeled for him, too.

Another man to watch is F.E. Sawyer. He is a River keeper on the Upper (Hampshire) Avon with wonderful sight & highly intelligent. He has been contributing to the *Salmon & Trout Magazine* (on my introduction) & to *Game & Gun* & he shd go far.

I was a bit concerned recently by a man on your side named Leisenring. He was apparently much impressed by my best book *Nymph Fishing for Chalkstream Trout* & he wrote me an enthusiastic letter & sent me a copy of a book he had written on American trout fly dressing & some quite nice lightly dressed specimens of his handiwork. These & the book I passed on to the Fly fishers club. But that is not all. A few weeks ago I had an almost hysterically affectionate letter from him describing how someone he called Charly had told him that I was dead & how terribly distressed he was & saying that he wrote Blacks, my publishers, to inquire & was so relieved when they said the announcement of my demise was premature that he went off & caught a bumper basket of trout.

Well I must reel up

With kindest regards and good wishes

Yours ever

G.E.M. Skues

P.S. Leisenring also sent me a copy of an American magazine called *Fortune* with a long & highly illustrated article on American trout fly dressing & a [?] about Theodore Gordon having written to Halford in 1890 to inquire the meaning of my nymph fishing articles & a part of a letter to Gordon from Halford (printed as a reply, but quite silent on the question). As a matter of fact I did not begin thinking of the matter till nearly 10 yrs later.

GEMS

January 16, 1947

My dear La Branche,

I gather from a letter I have had from Dr. Barton that you have been indulging in a gentle jibe at my expense over my criticism of the fly on which you took your first Itchen fish or a Surrey fowl. I wonder whether you recall the special conditions of that day & whether your use of a Surrey fowl was in any way dictated by them on that occasion. It was not till some while after that I let on the secret of your success on that occasion. It was blowing hard & creating quite a ruffle at the point where (as I told you) your 2¼ pounder lay and on several subsequent occasions on like conditions I have put on a big fly & have caught big fish up to 3lbs. & a visitor got one of 3lbs 12 oz. in a gale.

Kind Regards

Yours ever

GEMS

The book Skues mentions below, *Silk, Fur and Feather*, was eventually published in 1950.

April 27, 1947

My dear La Branche

Having somehow survived the recent prolonged & bitter winter little (apart from the lapse of months) the worse for wear I am trying to catch up with my correspondence & seem to be owing you a letter. It is two years now since growing shakiness of hands & break up of my feet put an end to both my flyfishing & my fly dressing, though not to my perennial interest in these subjects. I have presented most of my fly dressing materiel to the Fly fishers club— together with about 100 of my angling books to fill gaps in the Club Library & am endeavoring to dispose of the rest. It is now nearly 7 years since I visited the Club & I have only seen 2 or 3 members during that period.

During the worst of the Cold spell, which for Britain was exceptionally bitter I was moved to perpetrate the following Limerick

A Wicked old Sinner said "Well
We're assured it is warmer in Hell"
But if it grows colder
Before I'm much older
I'll be in position to tell.

Really it was rather savage weather for this country. . . .

The sporting newspaper called *Game & Gun* changed its name to the *Country Sportsman*. I was induced to subscribe for a year, but I find it has such a small proportion allotted to flyfishing that I do not propose to renew my subscription. There is no angling paper now any thing like as good as *The Field* before my clients sold it in 1919. The purchasers turned it into a picture paper, which the old staff regarded as a mistake—and I agreed with them.

A few months ago I was approached by a North Country angler who wanted to republish in book form a serial paper I had in the *Fishing Gazette* about 1927 called *Silk Fur & Feather*. It was all about fly dressing. I was prepared to agree, but the man kept proposing a series of additions by other hands, mostly unknown to me & as I did not want my work associated with writing which I might not approve I gather that the proposer has taken offence & has abandoned the project.

I hope this will find you flourishing.

Yours as ever

G.E.M. Skues

G.E.M. Skues died in 1949.

APPENDIX 3
INSECTS IMITATED BY LA BRANCHE FLIES

David Ledlie generously agreed to share his educated guesses on the identities of the insects imitated by La Branche's flies:

1. Whirling Dun: This would work for *Epeorus pleuralis* (Quill Gordon) or *Ephemerella subvaria* (Hendrickson).

2. Pale Evening Dun: Either *Stenonema vicarium* (March Brown) or *Stenonema fuscum* (Grey Fox)

3. Pink Lady: Perhaps *Stenonema ithaca*

4. Gold-Ribbed Hare's Ear: Probably *Ephemerella subvaria*

5. Flight's Fancy: *Ephemerella dorothea*

6. Silver Sedge: It sure doesn't look like a sedge—perhaps the mayfly *Ephoron leukon*

7. Willow: Perhaps just an attractor fly?

8. Mole: *Isonychia bicolor* and *sadleri*

These, obviously, are all guesses—but in the appropriate sizes the flies would imitate the aforementioned insects—as they are all quite common to Eastern trout waters.

David B. Ledlie

INDEX